PENGUIN BO

Self

Barry Dainton is professor of Philosophy at the University of Liverpool. He works in metaphysics and the philosophy of mind, and is influenced by current and predicted developments in science and technology. He is the author of three books: *The Phenomenal Self*, *Stream of Consciousness*, and *Time and Space*.

Self

What am I?

BARRY DAINTON

PENGUIN BOOKS

PENGUIN BOOKS

UK | USA | Canada | Ireland | Australia
India | New Zealand | South Africa

Penguin Books is part of the Penguin Random House group of companies
whose addresses can be found at global.penguinrandomhouse.com.

First published in 2014
This edition published 2016
001

Copyright © Barry Dainton, 2014

The moral right of the author has been asserted

Set in 12.5/14.75 pt Garamond MT Std
Typeset by Jouve (UK), Milton Keynes
Printed in Great Britain by Clays Ltd, St Ives plc

A CIP catalogue record for this book is available from the British Library

ISBN: 978–1–846–14620–6

www.greenpenguin.co.uk

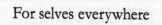
For selves everywhere

Contents

Acknowledgements   ix

Prologue   1

1. Dreams and Destinations   11

2. Routes to the Modern Soul   20

3. The Liberation of the Self   39

4. The Phenomenal and the Psychological   55

5. Selves, Powers and Subjects   70

6. Taking the Plunge   91

7. What Matters (and Other Matters)   113

8. The Place of Mind in the World   141

9. Future Selves   176

Epilogue: On Being Moved
(or Not) by Time   205

Notes   211

References   221

Index   225

Acknowledgements

My thanks to Galen Strawson, Andrew Crompton, Michael McGhee, Tom Winfield, Susan Bearder and Gwynneth Knowles for providing encouraging and helpful comments on earlier drafts, to Stephen Clark for urging me to keep thinking about simulations (and inadvertently supplying an epigram), and to Richard Gaskin, for reminding me not to neglect zombies. I am also grateful to everyone at Penguin for their enthusiasm for the project, and their help in bringing it to fruition. I am particularly grateful to Ananda Pellerin, not least for her many invaluable suggestions for streamlining the text and accelerating the telling of the tale.

In several parts of the book I have drawn on ideas developed in earlier writings – such as 'The Self and the Phenomenal', *Ratio* (2004), and 'Consciousness as a Guide to Personal Persistence' (co-author Tim Bayne), *Australasian Journal of Philosophy* (2005). Some material from 'On Singularities and Simulations', *Journal of Consciousness Studies* (2012), has found its way into the final sections of Chapter 9. I am grateful for permission to use this material here.

Prologue

You wake up feeling normal. It's only when you get to the bathroom that you notice there's something amiss. As you look in the mirror, you see your all-too-familiar face staring back . . . alas, it's not looking quite its best at this early stage of the day. A few moments pass before you notice something very peculiar: there are what look to be two short antennae sticking out of the top of your head. You give one of them a tug but there's no trace of give. Trying to come to terms with your new adornments, you brush back your hair and notice something else. On your forehead, just below your hairline, a rectangular area of skin is missing and has been replaced by what looks to be a piece of glass. Moving closer to the mirror, you see that the covering is fully transparent. You can't see far into the dark interior, but it is almost as if someone has fitted an inspection window into your head.

You leave the bathroom and go back to your bedroom, where you find an envelope on your dressing table. Clearly typed on its front are the words, 'YOUR MISSING BRAIN'. On opening the envelope – which you do with understandable haste – you find this message:

> Don't be alarmed! You don't need to know who we are, but you do need to know that we're the ones who have

kidnapped your brain. If you follow our instructions and do as we ask – you will receive an email from us shortly – your brain will be returned to you intact.

With rapidly mounting horror, you switch on your computer. While it's starting up you return to the mirror and take a closer look at the glass panel in your forehead. You use a small pen torch to shine a light inside, and you can now see what your skull contains – or doesn't contain. Your brain is indeed missing. In its place, at the centre of your otherwise empty cranium, is what looks to be a small electrical device, connected by bundles of electrical wires to your eyes, ears and down into your neck, to what must be the top of your spinal cord.

Your computer is now operational, and you soon find the promised email, including a link that you immediately click, and which reveals a video feed showing a vat of bubbling fluid. A brain is floating in the vat, connected via bundles of electrical cables to a computer. The accompanying audio commentary claims that the brain in the vat is in fact yours, and goes on to reveal the purpose of the antennae in your head: the electronic device in your skull, to which they are connected, is a radio transceiver, which is allowing electrical messages to flow back and forth between your body and your disembodied brain (wherever, exactly, *it* happens to be). These connections allow your body and brain to communicate in just the way they would – for all practical purposes – if your brain were sitting in your skull, and connected to your spinal cord and sensory organs in the normal way.

Worried though you are by the predicament you find

yourself in, the sheer strangeness of the situation is not lost on you. Your brain may be miles away from your head, but everything feels *exactly* as it normally does. Your senses are all working normally: if you pinch yourself it hurts; and your physical coordination is unimpaired. As it happens, you are a neuroscientist, and you are fully aware of the deep and pervasive ways in which our minds depend upon our brains – you are no stranger to the multifarious ways in which damage to our brains can impact upon our ability to function normally. In fact it's been many years since you felt anything less than 100 per cent confident in the notion that, for all intents and purposes, we *are* our brains. Since you do believe this, and you also believe that your brain is no longer in your body but floating inside the vat you can see on the computer monitor, this much is clear: you should feel *yourself* to be in the vat, along with your brain. After all, that's where your thinking is really taking place. But, try as you might, you can't really bring yourself to believe this. Or, at least, you can manage to believe that your brain is no longer in your head. But accepting this has no effect on where *you* seem to be located: you seem to be exactly where you are normally situated, i.e. at a point an inch or so behind your eyes and between your ears. You keep thinking, 'I'm not *here*, but *there*, in the vat!' several times over, willing yourself to believe it. But to no avail. You continue to have the vivid sense that you are indeed here, and that your brain is very much *elsewhere*.

This is an entertaining, albeit outlandish tale. But it's also a thought-provoking one. In fact, thought experiments of this sort play an important role in philosophy, and with good reason. There is much to be learned from situations which don't occur in real life, but which are nonetheless imaginable. For example, the thought experiment just outlined, the essentials of which derive from a famous article by the philosopher Daniel Dennett, raises a good many issues.[1] For one thing, it suggests that the relationship that exists between you and your brain is not as straightforward as you might have assumed. But it also brings into clear relief a simpler and more fundamental question: what *are* you?

That you exist is something you can be reasonably certain of – as certain as you can be of anything, surely. But what kind of thing are you, or any of the rest of us? When you think 'What am I?', who (or what) is doing the thinking? Few questions have greater resonance than this one, but down the ages few questions have proved to be more controversial, or as difficult to answer.

An initial response to the question, at least for anyone considering it in the twenty-first century, would be to say that it's obvious what we are: we are human beings, biological entities, members of the animal species *Homo sapiens*. Although this is the scientifically respectable answer, it is by no means the only possible one, or even the most popular. Many people think that, while of course we *have* biological bodies, we are more than just organisms. We also have souls that allow us to survive the death of our physical bodies. Just over 70 per cent of people in the United States believe they have a soul, and the figures are only slightly lower for the UK and Germany, while they are a good deal higher in Africa and India. Presumably most of these people would say that we don't just *have* souls, but that, fundamentally, we *are* souls. For whatever else it may be, for a soul to be worth having (or wishing for), it must be something which permits one's personality, intellect and conscious mental life to continue after the death of one's body. A soul of this sort is, in effect, a *mind*, and it's not something you 'have' in the way you have a sore foot; a soul is something you *are*.

In this book we will be looking at competing views of the self. Our central question will be: what *is* the self exactly? We will be weighing up the latest arguments for the idea that human beings have a self that is potentially separable from their bodies. Not a soul, *per se*, but a self that acts as the bearer of our mental states and capacities, and is capable of surviving the destruction of our physical bodies. The doctrine that we are essentially mental beings that are not inseparably bound to any particular human body has a long and distinguished history in philosophy as well as theology. Over the course of this book we will be assessing the purely philosophical case for thinking that we really are beings of this sort.

Debates about the nature of the self do not just matter in the abstract. How we conceive of ourselves is of profound importance to how we live and how we relate to others and the world around us. If we are in principle separable from our bodies, then with accelerating computer technology, and advances in neuroscience and medicine, it may not be long before such separations become practicable. In which case, it may not be long before we need to re-examine the ethical and metaphysical underpinnings of our legal frameworks relating to personhood. And, more generally, to reassess our assumptions regarding the kind of lives it is possible for people to lead.

When seeking to establish that we are *not* just our physical bodies, some of the arguments philosophers deploy derive from deep metaphysical doctrines relating to the nature of mental and physical things – and we'll be looking at some of these. But others are rooted in less esoteric considerations.

Many of us will have encountered stories or films in which advanced technology allows people to move from one body to another. In a typical 'body-swap' scenario, a brain-scanning device will take all the psychological states (i.e. memories, beliefs, personality traits, and so forth) from one brain and transfer them to another brain. In a similar vein, most of us have encountered the teleportation scenarios found in science fiction series such as *Star Trek*, whereby people can be 'beamed' from one location to another. Teleportation of this kind usually involves the teleportee's body being copied then destroyed before being rebuilt from new matter elsewhere.

Now, it is true that such technologies do not yet exist, and you may be sceptical about whether they ever will. But in the eyes of some philosophers this does not matter. If you and your current body are one and the same thing, then you and your current body could *never* come apart. The fact that we are able to envisage ourselves being transported in these sorts of ways suggests that these procedures may preserve all that is essential so far as our own survival is concerned. Since in mind transfers and teleportation we leave our original bodies behind, we should conclude that we *really are* separable from our original bodies. Moreover, by considering carefully what these procedures *do* conserve, we can isolate those features of our lives that are essential to our existence.

This line of argument features prominently in philosophical discussions relating to the self. In effect, its supporters aim to liberate us from our bodily confinement by appealing to *ways of moving people* that are possible or conceivable. Whether this strategy can succeed, and, if so, what sort of self it delivers, are issues we will be exploring.

Where should our investigations begin? Selves evidently are conscious, at least during their waking hours. Whatever else they may be, they are things which perceive their environments – by sight, hearing and touch – feel sensations in their bodies, think thoughts, reach decisions, recall their past experiences, undergo changes in their moods and emotions – to mention just some of the various forms of conscious experience most of us are fortunate enough to enjoy every day. But although consciousness is the most familiar thing in the world, and central to self-hood, in some respects it is a highly puzzling and contentious phenomenon.

The central puzzle is not what consciousness is like – we all know something of what it's like to be conscious – but how consciousness is related to the rest of the world and, more specifically, to our brains. Is consciousness a physical phenomenon, in the manner of mass, magnetism or electricity? Or is it something else entirely, something profoundly not physical? This has become known as 'the problem of consciousness', and it has loomed large in recent debates: over the past few decades there has been a huge surge of interest in the problem of consciousness across a wide range of disciplines, from psychology to neuroscience, quantum theory to contemporary art and dance, as well as philosophy. The obstacles to a scientific investigation of consciousness are certainly formidable. Science has progressed because it confined itself to studying objective, publicly observable phenomena such as the motions of the stars and planets, whereas consciousness is subjective: the only person with direct experience of what your experiences are like is *you*. Nonetheless, we will only have a complete scientific understanding of ourselves and the wider universe if we also have a scientific understanding of consciousness. No one thinks this understanding will be easy to achieve, but it is widely agreed that the task should not be postponed any longer.

We will be looking at why the problem of consciousness *is* so uniquely difficult – much of the answer lies in the conception of the physical world that emerged during the Scientific Revolution (and is still with us today). We will also be looking at some of the current best thinking on the relationship between the physical world and consciousness, i.e. at the most promising *solutions* to the problem of consciousness. These solutions, it turns out, have dramatically different implications for the nature of selves, their relationship to the wider world, and the sorts of transformations they could undergo.

It has often been claimed that cheating death is the deepest – if (perhaps) not the worthiest – motivation for believing that we have immortal souls. Thanks to anticipated advances in computer technology, some techno-optimists have argued that it won't be long before we are able to 'upload' ourselves to computer-sustained virtual paradises, where we will enjoy something approaching immortality. We will be scrutinizing these claims too, and considering how different conceptions of the nature of the self impact upon these hopes.

Might these virtual worlds affect the kind of things *we* are too? Suppose the techno-optimists are right, and the computers of the future will not only be able to generate virtual worlds populated by virtual inhabitants who are fully conscious, they will be able to create and sustain vast numbers of these worlds, with vast numbers of inhabitants, and with very little effort or cost. Given this, it might well be that the total number of computer-generated selves vastly outnumbers the total number of selves who are *not* computer-generated. In which case, it is more likely than not that *we* are among those living in computer-sustained virtual worlds. Is this really something we should be worried about? Does the hypothesis even make any sense? We will be examining these issues, and we will reach some surprising conclusions.

Taking a step back, it is worth noting that in some contemporary intellectual circles the doctrine that there exists anything resembling a self as traditionally conceived – a fundamentally mental thing that is in principle separable from its body – is widely assumed to have been wholly discredited, regardless of how most people might think of themselves. Indeed, the banishment of the self as traditionally conceived is sometimes seen as a hallmark of modernity, a view that discoveries in science and philosophy have rendered untenable. But I believe this assumption is simply wrong, or at least far too simplistic. While there is still much to be discovered about the relationship between our selves, our consciousness and the rest of reality – and we cannot yet be sure what the future will bring in the way of technological developments – as I hope to demonstrate, these gaps in our knowledge do not mean that valuable advances cannot be achieved, or that there isn't anything to be gained from the search itself. Not the least of these gains is a coherent conception of the self as a unified conscious subject, a conception that is entirely compatible with the advances of modern science.

But let us not get ahead of ourselves. We will launch our investigations by focusing on what might initially seem to be a more mundane issue. If we take it as a given that you exist, what sorts of journeys is it possible for you to undertake? What modes of transportation are open to you? What kinds of movements or spatial translations could you survive? I have already suggested that there is a close connection between these travel-related questions and the 'What am I?' issue. What will also emerge, when we probe the connection more deeply, is that when it comes to transportation, there are vitally important questions to which physics (or chemistry, or biology) cannot supply an answer, but to which *metaphysics* can.

1. Dreams and Destinations

The EU has been examining draft proposals for a hydrogen-fuelled hypersonic jet, the A2, which could take passengers from Brussels to Sydney in four and a half hours, rather than the full day our current generation of planes requires. This might sound impressive, but, even with a top speed of 4,000 mph, there is still plenty of room for improvement. Could a machine be built which could get us from Brussels to Sydney in half an hour? Or half a minute? The speed of sound is 343 metres per second, or about 1 mile every 5 seconds. The speed of light is about 300 *million* metres per second, or 186,000 miles every second. If the scientists are right, it's impossible for anything to travel faster than light, but how close could we get? Speed aside, the envisaged A2 is very noisy – it would only be allowed to achieve maximum speed over the sparsely inhabited polar regions – even worse, it doesn't have any windows. Clearly we could do better, but how much better? Is there an *ideal* method of transportation?

There's fast, and there's really fast

Sometimes the ideal mode of transportation is a riverboat trip down the Thames, or a leisurely stroll or bike ride, especially on a sunny summer's day. But let's assume what we're after is *speed*. Therefore, we want the method of transport to be as fast as possible, instantaneous even, as well as cheap, reliable and risk-free. Which brings us to the mode of transportation known as *teleportation*.

Several ways of implementing teleportation have been proposed by scientists, some more speculative than others. But one method in particular stands out as less speculative – and so more likely to be a practical proposition – and for this reason has been widely discussed by scientists, futurologists and philosophers. The procedure in question involves four stages:

1. You begin by stepping into the teleportation chamber and your body is subjected to a rapid but detailed scanning process. The data produced by the scan is safely stored on a computer.

2. Your body is then painlessly annihilated; the resulting matter and energy are safely disposed of (they don't get sent anywhere).

3. The information from the scan is transmitted to the desired destination by some very fast method of signalling using radio waves, laser beams and suchlike.

4. On arrival, this information is fed into an advanced 3D bio-printer, which (swiftly) creates a duplicate of your original body, just as it was at the moment of departure, in the 'receiving' teleport chamber. There are no

discernible physical or psychological differences between the original person and the newly created replica.

And then out you step, just as you were a few moments ago, as if nothing has happened.

Or so the story goes.

This procedure is often referred to as 'informational tele-portation', since only information – the coded data-pattern used to replicate you – is transmitted through space. Your body (don't forget) is annihilated at the outset, and the resulting waste products and energy are not preserved or sent anywhere. Your new body is constructed from entirely new materials stored in the 'receiving' teleport chamber. This informational variety of teleportation will be the type that we will be focusing on from now on (although other forms won't be ignored entirely).

Informational teleportation may not be instantaneous, but for most purposes it's pretty close. Travelling at the speed of light, a transit time of just a handful of seconds will be enough for you to be sent a million miles. You could cross the Atlantic in less than a second.

A scan of a human body that is sufficiently detailed to allow a (near) exact duplicate to be constructed will contain a sizable amount of information – vast by contemporary standards, but easily manageable, we can extrapolate, by future computational technologies. It could easily be the case that this data will be transmitted much as the data that makes up the internet is today: in the form of pulses of light sent along fibre-optic cables. As the writer Andrew Blum has noted, the internet is

> nearly everywhere ... a series of tubes. There are tubes beneath the ocean that connect London and New York. Tubes that connect Google and Facebook. There are buildings filled with tubes, and hundreds of thousands of miles of roads and railroad tracks, beside which lie buried tubes. Everything you do online travels through a tube. Inside those tubes (by and large) are glass fibres. Inside those fibres is light. Encoded in that light, is, increasingly, *us*. (Blum 2012: Prologue)

If optically based teleportation technology becomes a reality, it will be *us*, quite literally, who are being whisked from place to place at light-speed, temporarily encoded in pulses of light. In which case, tube-travel in the age of teleportation will be very different from what it is at the start of the twenty-first century.

But is it really *possible?*

You might think there is still a fanciful air about all of this, to put it mildly. However, anyone who is inclined to pessimism on this front should bear in mind Arthur C. Clarke's observation that a sufficiently advanced technology is indistinguishable from magic.[2] A couple of decades ago, the notion that something like the internet of today could even exist, let alone be accessed by a device as tiny as a modern smartphone, would have seemed like magic to most. The lesson is clear and sharp: it is dangerous to underestimate how fast technological developments might come.

But for those who may find the idea of travelling by teleportation an exciting prospect, and certainly an improvement on budget airlines, there is a second, more profound cause for concern. Even if teleportation is technologically possible, is it a process that our *selves* could possibly survive? Put another way, if you were to attempt to travel by this method, would the person who emerges from the cubicle at the destination be *you* or someone else entirely who merely resembles you very closely?

In most fictions in which teleportation is deployed (and in all video games) it is simply *stipulated* that the process is survivable. Disinclined as we are to break the flow of a promising storyline, many of us – initially at least – do not pause to worry whether this is actually the case. However, as we know, storytellers' stipulations can easily prove false. Think for example of the many tales featuring crystal balls which foretell the future, intelligent talking horses, or wizards who turn children into toads – or time travellers who change the past.

From physics to metaphysics

Since not everything that happens in stories is really possible, we would be wrong to conclude that teleportation is a genuine possibility – a way of *moving* people and not *killing* them – simply because it seems to work smoothly in games and movies. What we want to find out is whether or not the person who walks out of the teleport chamber is actually *you*, or merely a duplicate of you – i.e. someone else, a newly created person who happens to resemble you very closely.

Whether or not teleportation is survivable ultimately depends on the *kind of thing* that we are. Since philosophical investigations into the self are attempts to answer precisely this question, philosophers should have something to offer us in this regard. And it turns out that they do.

Let's leave the possibility that we might have non-physical souls to one side and work on the assumption that we are entirely physical things. There is a philosophical doctrine, called *animalism*, which states that we are indeed nothing more than biological organisms belonging to the species *Homo sapiens*. If we are ordinary material objects of this sort, what are the implications for the survivability (or otherwise) of teleportation?

If you were to pull apart all the constituent atoms of a cat and then scatter them to the four winds, you could be utterly certain of one thing: the cat has not survived. And what goes for cats goes for tables, chairs and other medium-sized material objects: none can survive total physical obliteration. Consequently, neither cats nor chairs can be moved from one place to another by informational teleportation. After all, in teleportation just about the very first thing which happens is the destruction – the total and utter annihilation – of the object that's placed in the teleport chamber. The resulting atoms and energy aren't sent anywhere; all that's transmitted elsewhere is the *information* resulting from the scanning process – the original atoms are simply dispersed. If the cat we carefully place into a teleport chamber goes out of existence shortly afterwards, the cat which emerges from the chamber at the other end of the line is obviously *not* the animal we started with. At best this cat is merely a replica of the original animal, fashioned from new materials. In which case informational teleportation is not a way of safely moving material objects; it is more akin to faxing, a way of moving data patterns around with a view to creating duplicates.

If cats can't survive teleportation, and if we are the same general kind of things as cats, i.e. living organisms, then neither can we. So if animalism is correct, attempting to travel by teleportation would be foolhardy in the extreme, for it would be fatal. However, animalism by no means offers the only philosophical view of what we are. There are several competing accounts, and some of these are a good deal more hospitable to travel by teleportation.

The most influential philosophical writing on the nature of the self in recent years is Derek Parfit's 1984 book, *Reasons and Persons*. In it, he provides a hypothetical scenario intended to teach us something about the kind of thing we are. It begins thus:

I enter the Teletransporter. I have been to Mars before, but only by the old method, a space-ship journey taking several weeks. This machine will send me at the speed of light. I merely have to press the green button. Like others, I am nervous. Will it work? I remind myself what I have been told to expect. When I press the button, I shall lose consciousness and then wake up at what seems a moment later. In fact I shall have been unconscious for about half an hour. The Scanner here on Earth will destroy my brain and body, while recording the exact states of all my cells. It will then transmit this information by radio. Travelling at the speed of light, the message will take three minutes to reach the Replicator on Mars. This will then create, out of new matter, a brain and body exactly like mine. It will be in this body that I wake up.

Though I believe that this is what will happen, I still hesitate. But then I remember seeing my wife grin when, at breakfast yesterday, I revealed my nervousness. As she reminded me, she has often been teletransported, and there is nothing wrong with *her*. I press the button. As predicted, I lose and then seem at once to regain consciousness, but in a different cubicle. Examining my new body, I find no change at all. Even the cut on my upper lip, from this morning's shave, is still there. (Parfit 1984: 201)

The teleportation process as presented here is survivable: it's Parfit who enters the chamber on Earth, and Parfit who emerges from the replicator at the other end. The passage also points to a significant implication of this mode of transportation. When teleporting, Parfit leaves his original body behind on Earth and regains consciousness a few minutes later in a new body on Mars. If, as Parfit maintains, the teleportation procedure is survivable, then it is possible for us to move from one body to another without any risk to our own existence.

Parfit's claim that teleportation is survivable is grounded

in his highly influential account of the persistence-conditions of people. According to Parfit, our personal survival requires a certain form of *mental continuity*, and – crucially – this form of continuity is preserved by informational teleportation: it does not require *material* continuity. Moreover, this form of mental continuity does not require us to have immaterial souls, or any other kind of mysterious, otherworldly properties.

Parfit's account of the self belongs to a tradition inaugurated by the English philosopher John Locke in the seventeenth century. In developing his own distinctive views, Locke was criticizing the account of the self defended by another influential thinker, the French philosopher René Descartes. In fact, the 'Cartesian' conception of the mind and self has been at the heart of philosophical discussions of these issues ever since it was elaborated some three and a half centuries ago. Descartes' answer to the 'What are we?' question is 'We are immaterial minds.' Here *immaterial* means 'not part of the physical world', rather than 'irrelevant'. If we are immaterial beings, then we do not have any physical constituents, and we do not exist in physical space. We have bodies that exist in the physical world, but we are not the same things as our bodies.

Although few philosophers these days think this account is entirely correct, few would deny the power and appeal of Descartes' way of thinking, or his continued influence on current debates. In the next chapter we will be looking at those aspects of Descartes' doctrines that still have contemporary relevance.

2. Routes to the Modern Soul

Immaterial souls have been popular for millennia – and it's no surprise, offering as they do a route to life eternal in the paradise promised by many religions. If you are going to survive the death and destruction of your body, it will be a good deal easier if you are an entity that is distinct from your body, and the soul fits the bill. But, if we set wishful thinking and religious considerations aside, what other reasons could there be for thinking that we are immaterial entities?

Many of the most potent and influential philosophical arguments for the non-physicality of the self were offered by René Descartes at the start of the era that produced modern philosophy (an era that runs roughly from the fifteenth to the eighteenth centuries). In fact Descartes is often called the father of modern philosophy. If the notion that selves *are* minds – physical or non-physical – is commonplace in contemporary philosophy, it is largely because of the compelling case Descartes put forward for viewing them as such.

The reasons which led Descartes to exclude the self from the physical world are powerful – more so than is often recognized – and they still have force today. Although most contemporary philosophers reject Descartes' dualistic view of mind and body, most would also agree that the problems he raised for understanding *how* beings which possess conscious intelligence can be a part of the material world have yet to be solved.

Demons and vats

Descartes is probably best known for a thought experiment introduced in his *Meditations on First Philosophy* (1641), which is familiar to all students of philosophy – more often than not it is the first text they are asked to read. Descartes invites us to consider the radical hypothesis that our experience does not derive from perceptual contact with the external world, as we normally suppose. Instead, our experience is being completely controlled by a powerful and malicious Demon, who is intent on misleading us as to our real condition. In effect, the world that is presented to us in our experience is nothing but a hallucination induced by this Demon. In more modern versions of the scenario – along the lines of the missing brain tale – you are reduced to the condition of a brain-in-a-vat, a brain that is wholly unaware of its true condition because mad scientists are electrically stimulating your sensory nerves, providing you with illusory experiences of a normal body and environment. A similar version of essentially the same scenario is explored in the *Matrix* movies.

The challenge Descartes laid down is simple: can you prove that your current experience is *not* being produced by such a Demon?

It is not easy to do. Yes, you can see the wall in front of

you, you can also reach out and feel its reassuring solidity, but, according to Descartes' alternative hypothesis, these experiences are among those being produced by the Demon and so are not to be trusted. When you look into a mirror and see a human being staring back, you cannot conclude that you *are* a human being, for these experiences are also Demon-produced. It's also true that you don't just *see* your body, you can *feel* it: you can run your hands over your limbs and touch your face with your fingers. But it's no use: all *these* experiences are produced by the Demon as well.

Unless you can come up with a compelling reason as to why the sceptic's argument is flawed, you can't be sure that you even have a body. You might be an entirely non-physical thing – a thing whose true nature you cannot comprehend in your current condition, a thing which just happens to be hallucinating that it has a human form.

The real purpose of the demonic thought experiment wasn't to establish a more extensive scepticism than the world had hitherto seen: far from it. Descartes' stated aim in the *Meditations* was to distinguish what we *really* know from what we merely *think* we know, with a view to re-establishing our framework of knowledge on solid foundations.

Subjects and appearances

Descartes argued that unless you can rule out the possibility that your experiences aren't being produced in some deviant and misleading way you cannot be sure that reality is as your experience suggests. You seem to have a coffee cup in your hands, but you can't be certain that you really do.

Despite all this, Descartes did think you could be certain of one thing: that *you* are now having your current thoughts and experiences. Hence his famous phrase, '*Cogito, ergo sum*', 'I think, therefore I am'. The message being that irrespective of how things really are, whether you are being controlled by a Demon or are a brain-in-a-vat, since you are thinking these very thoughts (or reading these lines) you can at least be certain that you exist and that you are currently having these experiences and thoughts, even if you don't really know (for absolutely certain) where or even what you are.

That's not all. You can also be certain of something about your own nature. Whatever else you may be – human, alien, angel, hallucinating robotic machine – you are *the kind of thing that is able to have experiences*. In other words, you are a 'conscious subject'. This may not seem like much, but it is certainly something – and it is something solid that Descartes believed we could build on.

Descartes' thought experiment also teaches us something about the nature of our experiences, namely that their *subjective character* – what they are like to have *as* experiences – is to a surprising degree independent of goings-on in the external world. You might assume that you can only have the sort of experience you have when you look at a brilliant red rose by actually looking at some red roses, and, hence, that experiences of this kind can only exist if red roses exist. Of course, anyone who has in real life hallucinated seeing a red rose, or anything else for that matter, would not need Descartes to tell them that this assumption is incorrect. What Descartes' argument allows us to appreciate is that the nature of *all* our experience is similarly independent of external reality.

From the fact that fully realistic hallucinations are possible, it follows that our perceptual experience is only a fallible guide to reality. Does it also follow, from this alone, that experience can't itself be physical in nature? No, and Descartes didn't claim that it did. What he did claim was that to know the full story about the relationship between the physical and the experiential we first need to understand the true nature of both. As we will see, Descartes' conviction that the mental couldn't be physical is ultimately rooted in his conception of the underlying nature of the physical world.

Scientific revolutionaries

In Descartes' day the division between science and philosophy (or philosophy and theology) had yet to be clearly drawn, and the greater part of Descartes' intellectual efforts went into what we would now call science, rather than philosophy, theology or anything else. He worked on optics – he discovered the law of refraction – and the physics of moving bodies. He is also credited with discovering the principle of inertia in its modern form. But Descartes' interests weren't confined to physical science.

He also performed ground-breaking work in mathematics, where he found a way of connecting geometry and algebra: most of us have encountered 'Cartesian coordinates' in school long before we are introduced to any of his philosophy.

Descartes was one of a number of influential thinkers – along with Copernicus, Kepler, Brahe, Galileo, Pascal, Torricelli, Huygens, Hooke, Leibniz and Newton – who would successfully initiate what would later become known as the Scientific Revolution. What made the 'revolutionary' label appropriate were not just the radically new kinds of theories being proposed, but these thinkers' attitudes to the past.

In the period preceding the Scientific Revolution, the dominant way of thinking about the natural world in the West was called 'Scholastic' science, a refined (and Christianized) way of thinking pioneered 1,800 years earlier in the fourth century BC by Aristotle, the founder of the Lyceum in Athens, tutor to Alexander the Great and Plato's most eminent ex-pupil.

For Aristotle, the universe is very much as it appears to us to be. The Earth is utterly motionless, sitting at the centre of the universe, and the sun, stars and planets all rotate around it. The most basic kinds of physical things are the primary elements (earth, fire, water, air) and material substances, the prime examples of which are living organisms: cats, dogs, horses, fish, trees and the like. Physical things are all made of physical stuff, but beyond that they differ enormously: cats are very different from fish, fish are very different from trees, and trees are very different from hunks of rock. What explains these differences?

Aristotle held that all physical things are *hylomorphic*, i.e. combinations of basic material stuff and so-called 'substantial forms'. A dog and an oak tree are both composed of material stuff – in different proportions of the four basic elements – but the most decisive difference between them lies in the active principle of organization, the *form*, which animates and bestows qualitative properties on the matter composing them. Taken by itself, basic (or 'prime') matter is utterly inert and incapable of constituting anything of interest. It is only when it is infused with (or possessed by) a controlling form that it can constitute things of the sorts we are familiar with. All the different types of things to be found in nature have their own distinctive form. We are distinctive by virtue of possessing *human forms*, which are responsible for our distinctive intellectual abilities.

These rational human forms were how the Scholastics thought of souls. While they were committed to the view that our souls are destined to be reunited with our bodies after the Day of Judgement, the Scholastics also believed it is possible for souls and their bodies to come apart: when we die, our souls can expect to spend some time *without* our bodies, in purgatory. Quite what life is like for a disembodied soul provoked considerable controversy in medieval theological circles.

By the fifteenth century, Aristotelianism had largely stagnated. On many fronts our understanding of the natural world had made little real progress for centuries.

Those who believed radical progress was possible – revolutionaries such as Galileo, Kepler and Descartes – also believed that a necessary first step was the overthrow of Scholastic science and metaphysics. Since this would mean rejecting the hylomorphic system, we would need – as Descartes was well aware – a new conception of our own natures.

The new worldview

It was with this broader revolutionary purpose in mind that we find Galileo arguing, quite brilliantly, that the Earth might really be moving at vast speeds around the sun even though it doesn't seem to be. Among other things, he pointed out that the passengers in the cabin of a fast-moving ship aren't aware of the ship's motion when they interact with their immediate surroundings – the wine in a glass remains flat and still, smoke from extinguished candles rises straight up, butterflies can fly around in their normal fashion. Motion, it seems, has very little effect on things which move – a phenomenon that is all the more striking in the faster modes of transport, such as today's trains and jet liners.

Cosmology aside, when it came to the nature of the Earth and what is to be found upon it, the scientific pioneers were equally radical. Most of them subscribed to a 'mechanical' or 'corpuscularian' worldview, according to which the behaviour of everything is explainable in terms of the laws governing the motions and interactions of extremely small (invisible) material particles. On this new view, material things are composed of nothing but matter, and objects behave as they do solely because of the physical laws governing their constituent particles.[3] Aristotle's once-indispensable 'forms' were dismissed as redundant obstacles to a deep understanding of the natural world. Living things such as trees and birds do differ radically in their appearances and patterns of behaviour, both from one another and from *non*-living things, yet these differences are not to be explained by any animating forms but solely and simply in terms of basic physical constituents and natural laws.

In making these claims Galileo and Descartes knew there was much still to discover about what matter is composed of at the smallest scales. But even so, these early scientific pioneers were confident that their general programme was the way forward. And, as we now know, it turns out they were correct.[4]

From science to soul

For supporters of the mechanical worldview, there is a very real sense in which physical things of all kinds *are* machines. How well a clock manages to tell the time depends on the mechanical parts it possesses and how well these are integrated. A living animal isn't composed of cogs, springs and gearwheels, as Descartes, an amateur vivisectionist, appreciated. But an animal is entirely composed of smaller physical parts, and the ways in which it can behave depends solely on how these parts are put together. In fact, Descartes thought it likely that animal bodies are hydraulic systems, powered by fluids running through very fine tubes.

Yet he found it hard to see how a system powered by physical mechanisms of this sort could possess the boundless creativity that is the hallmark of genuine intelligence – the sort of intelligence that humans possess. The Scholastics had a solution (of sorts) to this problem: we are *not* mere machines, for the matter which makes up our bodies is inhabited (or possessed) by a rational soul, so *of course* we are intelligent rational beings. However, for those who adopt the mechanical world-view and reject animating forms, the problem of the source of our intelligence looms large. Seeing no alternative solution, Descartes felt obliged to conclude that our intelligence cannot reside in a *physical* thing at all, and hence that our minds themselves cannot be physical.

The problem of understanding how a mere physical thing (such as a human brain) could possess intelligence has not gone away, for the mechanical view of living things is still with us; it underpins modern biology and medicine. But Descartes had another – better and deeper – reason for suggesting that our minds are non-physical, a reason connected not to intelligence, but to *consciousness*.

Consider the properties of an iron cube and an orange. There are differences in shape: one is more or less spherical, the other cubic. There are also differences in colour and texture: the cube is silvery-grey and smooth, the other orange-coloured and somewhat rougher to the touch. And of course there are significant differences in weight and hardness. One of the more far-reaching insights of thinkers such as Galileo, Descartes and Locke during the early days of the Scientific Revolution was the realization that, while some of these properties belong to the objects themselves, others are much more likely to be a product of *our responses to* the objects when we perceive them. Properties such as size, mass and shape are intrinsic to the objects – they have these whether we are present and perceiving them or not – whereas properties such as warmth (as a felt quality), texture (ditto), sound and colour only exist as aspects of our experience.

Galileo illustrated this point by asking us to consider whether the tingle triggered by a tickly feather is a feature of the feather itself. If you were to stroke a marble statue with a feather, would a tickling sensation be produced? Of course not. The tingle is a sensation, felt on our skin, the feather merely possesses the capacity to provoke or cause the tingling sensation. The feather doesn't carry the tingle around on its tip, waiting for us to sense it. The same holds, albeit far less obviously, for colour. Although colours *seem* to be located on the surfaces of the objects we see, in fact they only exist as features of our experiences. Colours only exist in sensory states that are triggered by light being reflected from objects and hitting (and stimulating) our eyes. Such is also the case for sound-properties, and sensations of texture and warmth.

In the terminology that John Locke would make standard in his *Essay Concerning Human Understanding* (1689), features such as mass and shape are *primary* properties, whereas colour, sound and texture (as felt) are *secondary* properties. Physical things, considered as they are in themselves, possess only properties of the primary variety. Hence for Locke, and the many who later followed in his footsteps, a rose is red not because its surface is covered with red-as-we-perceive-it (for it isn't); it is red because of the kind of visual experiences that light reflected from roses tends to produce in human perceivers.

What we know as sounds, colours, itches, pains and tingles are now called *phenomenal properties*, or *qualia*. And it is now believed that the primary properties of physical

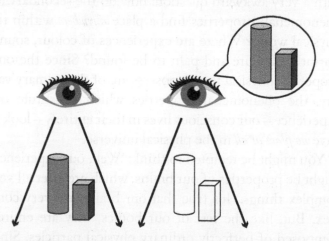

On the left is how (visual) perception seems to be: we are directly aware of the colourful objects in our environments. On the right is the post-Scientific Revolution view. Material objects are not covered in colour in the way they seem to be. We perceive external objects only indirectly, via the intervening visual images – which *do* possess colour, and which exist in our minds.

things include electric charge, spin and a few others, in addition to size, shape, mass and motion. But the basic picture remains much the same, as does the crucial message: many of the properties that we naturally assume are to be found in the external environment – e.g. in the case of colours, on the surfaces of physical things – are in fact to be found only in our own minds.

Descartes was the first to grasp the full significance of this new way of understanding things.

If, as he believed, the fundamental physical properties are restricted to the primary properties – mass, charge, shape, size, motion, spin, and so forth – then we are confronted with a very awkward question: how do the secondary (or phenomenal) properties find a place *anywhere* within the physical world? Where are experiences of colour, sound, warmth, pleasure and pain to be found? Since the only properties physical things possess are of the primary variety, the phenomenal properties which constitute our experience – our conscious lives in their entirety – look to have *no place at all* in the physical universe.

You might be tempted to think: 'Well, our experiences might be properties of our brains, which are after all very complex things.' It's true that our brains are very complex. But, like the rest of our bodies, they are entirely composed of perfectly ordinary physical particles. Since these particles only possess primary properties, our experiences cannot be properties of these physical things either. So it looks as though we have no option but to conclude that our experiences are simply not part of the physical world.

This is precisely the step that Descartes took. What we can now appreciate is that he had powerful *scientific* reasons for so doing.

The Cartesian soul

By this point Descartes has successfully established that *experiences* are distinct from anything that is physical. To complete the picture just one further element is needed: we need to introduce the *owner* or *subject* of these experiences.

Descartes conceived of the world in terms of objects and the properties which they possess. Ordinary physical properties such as 'heavy' or 'flat' or 'dented' can't exist all by themselves; they are necessarily properties (or modes) of an object – there is always some*thing* which is heavy or flat or dented (or all three). The same applies at the mental level. Individual experiences, e.g. a particular twinge of pain, or a feeling of sadness, the seeing of a red rose, the thinking of a thought, are not independent, free-standing things, capable of existing all by themselves. Rather, they are things which *happen to* someone or something. To put it another way, they are items which are *had by* someone, their subject or owner. Just as physical properties are possessed by physical things, so too will mental properties be possessed by mental things – or mental *substances*, as Descartes called them.

If experiences are not parts or properties of the physical world, the substances to which they belong can hardly be part of the physical world either. Since we know that our experiences are things which belong to us, it is natural to conclude that *we* are those substances. We are thus led to the conclusion that we are non-physical or immaterial things. These immaterial, mental substances are Cartesian souls. Since they are not parts of the physical world, they have no physical properties: they do not extend through space; they have no mass or momentum. Descartes believed these souls were simple or *atomic* in nature. Only something atomic (or free of parts) could be unified in the deep and distinctive way our consciousness is, or so he argued.

What sorts of mental properties do these souls possess? In his Second Meditation, Descartes tells us that a thinking substance is 'A thing that doubts, understands, affirms, denies, is willing, is unwilling, and also imagines and has sense perceptions.' So the mental lives of Cartesian souls do not consist solely of sensory or perceptual experiences; they also include memories and mental images, the conscious thoughts we think, the power to solve problems, the experience of understanding when we listen to others, or read their words, along with decisions and volitions. By virtue of possessing the complete range of mental properties and capacities, Cartesian souls are fully fledged *minds* in the contemporary sense of the term – indeed, Descartes is often credited with introducing the term 'mind' into the philosophical literature.

If we view souls as minds of this sort, and take ourselves to be these souls/minds, then, in principle at least, the absence of a physical body need not compromise one's ability to enjoy a rich mental life in the hereafter. Precisely what one experiences in heaven (or hell) will depend on what God decides, but the potential is there for one to have all sorts of wondrous thoughts and experiences, and to keep on having them forever. As the Cartesian view gained ground, the idea that one needed a physical body to enjoy an afterlife also lost purchase, and people increasingly assumed that they would spend their time in heaven (or hell) as immaterial things. Of course, we might well *seem* to have bodies in the afterlife – in line with certain passages in the Bible – but after Descartes it was possible to suppose that the appearance of a body could exist in the absence of anything physical at all.[5]

Transworld interaction

Though Descartes thought of souls as non-physical, they are by no means wholly separate and independent of the physical world. For Descartes also holds that minds and their bodies causally interact. Although this makes for difficulties – as we'll see later on – his position is the more plausible for it.

When we open our eyes, what we see – and hence the visual experience we have – depends on what is out there in the world before our eyes. Perceptual experience is a prime example of physical-to-mental causation, with happenings in the physical world producing experiences in our minds. But this is only half the story, for there is also mental-to-physical causation: if you decide to raise your arm, this mental event (a decision) results in a physical event (the movement of your arm). Provided these causal connections are in place, you will be able to interact with the physical world even if in reality your mind (and self) is located elsewhere.

Since your mind is located *nowhere at all* (if Descartes is right), its ability to produce changes in the physical world is a quite remarkable one. However, one aspect of Descartes' conception of how mind and body interact will seem entirely familiar, and not at all noteworthy:

> I further notice that the mind does not receive the impressions from all parts of the body, but only from the brain . . . when I feel a pain in my foot, my knowledge of physics teaches me that this sensation is communicated by means of nerves dispersed through the foot, which, being extended like cords from there to the brain . . .
> (*Discourse on Method*, 1637: 76)

Here we see that Descartes' conception of how the mind and body interact differs very little from the contemporary view: irrespective of whether or not the mind *is* the brain, the mind interacts with the body *via* the brain and the nerves which connect it to the rest of the body. Descartes took a further step and speculated that the causal exchange between the immaterial mind and brain takes place in the pineal gland, which sits right at the heart of the brain, and isn't divided into two parts in the manner of the cerebral hemispheres. This proved not to be the case – we now know that the pineal gland doesn't serve a particularly important purpose – but it wasn't a bad idea at the time.

By this point a thought along these lines may have crossed some people's minds:

> Isn't the notion that we are non-physical things open to an obvious objection that hasn't yet been discussed? Our experience is such that it's just obvious that we exist in this world, in the midst of physical things spread through physical space. How could our experience be as it is if in reality we are immaterial inhabitants that don't actually exist in the physical world?

However, the dualist has nothing to fear here. As the Dennett-inspired story of the missing brain we encountered in the Prologue very effectively demonstrates, the actual location of the thing which actually carries or sustains our minds is of no consequence when it comes to where we *seem* to be, subjectively. If the character of our experience is perfectly normal, we will appear to be located in our bodies, and, more specifically, in our heads, even if the thing producing our experience is located elsewhere. And of course this applies irrespective of whether the thing in question is a brain that has been envatted in a distant laboratory or an immaterial soul. Provided the connections between brain (or soul) and body are such as to allow them to communicate in the normal ways, so that our sensory experience and abilities to control our bodies are unaffected, then so too is our subjective sense of self-location.

So, strange as it may seem, we needn't actually *be* in a world in order for it to seem as though we are.

Descartes' conception of the self is clear and distinctive, and has a good deal to offer to anyone interested in the possibility of surviving the death of their bodies. If Descartes is right, it is possible for you to come apart from your body because they are distinct things that are composed of fundamentally different kinds of ingredients: your body is physical but *you* are an immaterial mind. For you and your body to be separated, nothing very dramatic has to happen: if the causal connections linking you to your body are severed, you and your body will go their separate ways.

However, Descartes' conception of how selves are related to their bodies (and the rest of the world) is a radical one. His mind–body dualism has powerful motivations – it certainly isn't easy to comprehend how our consciousness can be physical – but it is also controversial. Are there ways of loosening the ties between self and body without committing ourselves to Cartesian dualism? Yes there are, as we shall see in the next chapter.

3. The Liberation of the Self

So far we have encountered two of the main answers to the 'What are we?' question. One view, associated with scientifically educated, contemporary common sense, is that we are biological beings, in the specific form of human animals. Another view, held by Descartes and many other metaphysicians in recent centuries, is that we are fundamentally our *minds*, and these minds are non-physical, soul-like substances. A third answer can be found by looking at the theories put forward by John Locke.

Locke was one of the more influential figures of both the Enlightenment and the Scientific Revolution. His defence of empiricism was as important as his work in political philosophy, where he is regarded as one of the founders of modern liberalism. In days when it was dangerous to do so, he opposed absolute monarchy, advocated religious tolerance and the separation of Church and State. Thomas Jefferson wrote that 'Bacon, Locke and Newton ... I consider them as the three greatest men that have ever lived, without any exception, and as having laid the foundations of those superstructures which have been raised in the Physical and Moral sciences.' Locke also had some radical things to say on the topic of the self.

In 1694 he published a second edition of his *Essay*

Concerning Human Understanding (first published in 1689). To an already monumental work he added a chapter on 'Identity and Diversity'. What Locke had to say here revolutionized philosophical thinking about the self.

In this chapter we will be concentrating on Locke's main theses regarding the self, and I will show how they remain relevant to this day.[6] Although impressive in many respects, Locke's theory is also problematic, and, as we shall see, one of the leading contemporary accounts of the self – the 'Neo-Lockean' or 'psychological' view – arises directly from attempts to solve these problems. And, as it happens, the psychological theory also has some implications for our question of whether or not teleportation would be survivable.

Rational parrots, vampires and companionable aliens

Locke had two important and enduring insights. The first is that anyone who seeks to understand the nature of selves by focusing exclusively on human beings is overlooking something crucial.

Think for a moment of a favourite (or detested) non-human character in sci-fi or fantasy. There are any number to be found in the movies, ranging from E. T. to Wall-E. In *Star Trek* there are the too-logical Vulcans and the android Commander Data. In *The Lord of the Rings* we have human-like elves and dwarves, but also the Ents – a race of intelligent, talking (and mobile) trees.

Similarly, the creatures of the night to be found in the many vampire tales are non-human, and the many humans who are turned into vampires cease to be human.

These characters may only be fictional, but they are nonetheless philosophically interesting because it is easy – natural, even – to think of them as *people*, even though they are unequivocally non-human. They may be very different from us in some respects, but they are conscious beings that experience the world in much the way we do, and have thoughts and feelings. They are intelligent (often more so than us), and can talk, argue and reason. Moreover, they are evidently moral agents in their own right. Clearly, in an important sense these beings are *the same kind of thing* as us, even though in many respects they are very different from us.

Locke appreciated this fact and used the term 'person' to refer to the (potentially very broad) spectrum of beings that might fall into this category. His own best-known example of a person of the non-human variety is a rational parrot, able to philosophize and talk intelligently on a variety of topics. The parrot is definitely non-human, but, in Locke's eyes, it is definitely a person. We are persons as well, but so too are Vulcans, vampires, elves and Ents – along with E. T. and Wall-E. *Person* is a far broader category than *human being* – there are human persons, but there are non-human persons. Or, as Locke himself puts it, a person is 'a thinking intelligent being, that has reason and reflection, and can consider itself as itself, the same thinking thing, in different times and places; which it does only by that consciousness which is inseparable from thinking' (*Essay* 2.27.9).

For Locke a person is *anything* which has the mental capacities he lists: the ability to have experiences, to feel, to think and reason intelligently, and to be aware of oneself *as* a conscious subject which has existed for some time, as one that has a past. It may be that human beings are the only beings that have these mental capabilities and, if so, we are alone in the Universe – or at least there are no other people to keep us company. But if on some distant planet there are aliens that meet these conditions – no matter how bizarre their physical appearance by human standards – then they too count as persons. In our own age it's not difficult for us to imagine a future in which computers come to possess the attributes required for personhood.

Now we know what a 'person' is for Locke, but a question we have yet to address is their nature. Are persons wholly material things, or a combination of (potentially separable) material and immaterial parts? On this question Locke was agnostic. He believed it quite possible – even probable – that Descartes was right in claiming that (in this life at least) we are immaterial soul-substances that are bound to physical bodies. But he did not commit himself to this view. For Locke also held that our understanding of our own natures and the physical world is very limited, and he was open to the notion that matter, suitably configured, might possess the capacity to be conscious. Or, as he put it, there is no inherent contradiction in supposing that God could, 'if he pleased, give to certain systems of created senseless matter, put together as he thinks fit, some degree of sense, perception and thought' (*Essay* 4.3.6).

Locke's willingness to consider the possibility of *thinking matter* was received with horror by many of his contemporaries, but it would later be viewed as prophetic.

Personal identity

Locke subscribed to a very contemporary-sounding conception of the identities of plants and animals: both are dynamic, self-organizing systems of material particles. What makes for the difference between an apple tree and a tiger are the particular *ways* in which their constituent particles are organized. Locke followed Galileo, Descartes and the other scientific revolutionaries in rejecting the substantial forms proposed by Aristotle and the Scholastic philosophers of the Middle Ages. But what of the identity of *persons*, that new category of entity which Locke argues – very compellingly – that we should recognize?

In more recent times, the issue we are now broaching is known as the problem of 'personal identity over time', or simply the problem of 'personal identity'. In more general and precise terms, the question is this:

If a person P_1 at time t_1 and a person P_2 at a later time t_2 are numerically identical, how must P_1 and P_2 be related?

Here, 'numerically identical' means *one and the same entity*. This sense of identity is distinct from 'qualitative identity', as it is often called. Two objects are qualitatively identical if they are indistinguishable, i.e. they have exactly the same properties. Since most objects change their properties over time – we certainly do – earlier and later objects that are numerically identical will usually not be qualitatively identical.

Now, if you believe that you are a human animal, if some later person is going to be you, this person will have to be numerically the same animal as you. If you believe that you are an immaterial soul, then, if you are going to exist at some later time, a soul that is numerically identical with your current soul will have to exist at that time. Locke did not categorically reject the existence of immaterial souls, and he certainly believed human animals exist, but, crucially, he rejected both of these accounts of personal identity.

To paraphrase his view, what is needed for an earlier and a later person to be one and the same is for that later person to be *mentally continuous* with the earlier person. Or, to put it slightly differently, they must share the same *mental life*. Mental continuity makes for sameness of person irrespective of what else occurs.

The 'irrespective of what else occurs' here has to be interpreted literally. Locke insists that, if your mental life continues, but in doing so it is sustained by a succession of different physical beings, then your identity is entirely unimpaired; it is not affected or diluted in the least. He supports this claim with a variety of thought experiments. Perhaps the most famous is a case involving a high-born prince and a lowly cobbler. Suppose one day, thanks to some magical or miraculous intervention, the distinctive psychological traits of the two are switched. As a conse-

44

quence, the person who wakes in the cobbler's cottage (and body) has all the memories of the prince: he believes himself to be the prince; when he looks in the mirror he is shocked by his appearance, and wonders how on earth he ended up in this unfamiliar hovel. Simultaneously, someone is waking up in the prince's bedroom who is similarly astonished to find themselves in unfamiliar surroundings, and in an unfamiliar body. Isn't it obvious that the two have exchanged bodies? For Locke, it is.

Locke's prince-cobbler case is an early example of the mind-transfer or body-swap scenario that will be familiar to most of us from numerous science fiction stories, films and TV shows, such as *Quantum Leap*, *Total Recall* and *Avatar*.

Liberation from the soul

Locke's account of what makes for personal identity has radical consequences. Remember, Locke's key claim here is that mental continuity makes for sameness of person *irrespective of what else occurs*. If we can conceive of the same mental life – and hence the same person – being sustained by a succession of different physical substances, can't we also envisage the same mental life being carried by a succession of different *mental* substances? Locke argues that both scenarios are equally imaginable. Body-swaps are possible, but so too are soul-swaps.

As far as Locke was concerned, our knowledge of immaterial souls is so limited that anyone arguing that our mental lives *are* tied down to a single soul is in a very weak position. Hence his challenge: anyone who holds that our conscious mental lives occur within immaterial soul-substances 'must show why personal identity cannot be preserved in the change of immaterial substance, or variety of immaterial substances, [just] as well as animal identity is preserved in the change of material substances' (*Essay* 2.27.12). He was confident that no such demonstration would be forthcoming, and many subsequent philosophers – notably, and influentially, Immanuel Kant – have come to the conclusion that Locke was right.

In putting forward this substance- and soul-independent approach to the self, Locke was motivated by the conviction that the account he was offering was more plausible – more believable – than the alternatives. In this I think he was correct. But we know he was also motivated, in part, by religious considerations. Many Christian churches hold that on the Day of Judgement (which Locke himself referred to as 'the Great Day, wherein the secrets of all hearts will be laid open') the souls of the dead will be reunited with their bodies. But this gives rise to some awkward questions. If our bodies are made up of constantly changing swarms of atoms, which atoms will God use when he re-creates our bodies? What if the atoms aren't available because they also form part of *someone else's* body? In the light of these hard-to-resolve problems there were clearly advantages to having an account of personal identity that does not require sameness of physical body.

This point aside, what is of particular interest to us is the way Locke manages to offer a positive account of what we are while remaining agnostic on so many *other* basic metaphysical issues. Is consciousness physical or non-physical in nature? If consciousness is non-physical, is it housed in an immaterial substance, or not? So far as Locke is concerned, the answers to these questions do not matter in the least when it comes to answering the questions 'What are persons?' and 'Under what conditions will an earlier and later person be one and the same?' As we have seen, for Locke a person is a rational, self-conscious being, irrespective of what it is made of, and earlier and later persons are numerically identical if they are mentally continuous.

Being able to solve the problem of personal identity, while remaining neutral on the issue of the relationship between consciousness and the physical world, is an impressive and valuable feat, given that this issue remains as controversial today as it was in Locke's time.

Problems for Locke

Locke's claim that mental continuity is by itself sufficient for our continued existence, irrespective of what sustains it, looks like an advance over theories which bind the self to particular objects. But what precisely does 'mental continuity' amount to? Unfortunately, Locke himself didn't provide us with a great deal of guidance. In several passages he does say that it is 'sameness of consciousness' that makes for sameness of self.

At any given time we are aware of – we are *conscious of* – our current experiences: everything that we are perceiving, thinking and feeling. However, our consciousness – our awareness – of our own lives is not confined to what we are presently experiencing, far from it.

Just think of all those earlier experiences you enjoyed (or suffered) which you are still able to remember more or less vividly: what you experienced on your first day at school (or your last), what you saw (smelt, heard) on your first trip abroad, or your last birthday, and so on. Most of us can't remember everything that we have experienced earlier in our lives, but most of us can remember a great deal. Those past experiential episodes which we are able to remember also count as things we can be 'conscious' of, in Locke's sense – and so all those past experiences that we can remember also belong to us. Hence Locke's claim that 'as far as this consciousness can be extended backwards to any past action or thought, so far reaches the identity of that person.'

Our personal memories of our own earlier actions and experience *do* provide us with what might plausibly be called a consciousness of our own pasts, and in subsequent years Locke was widely considered to be defending a 'memory theory' of our identity over time. The theory has some plausibility, but critics were soon to develop serious objections to it.

Our memories are important to us, certainly, but are they really necessary to our continued existence? Suppose that tomorrow you receive a blow to your head, and the resulting minor brain damage results in severe amnesia, so severe that you can no longer recall anything of your previous life. Since the brain damage is relatively minor, the resulting mental changes are confined to the loss of your personal memories, while your capacity for experience, reason and language are unaffected. Would you regard this misfortune as fatal? If the same happened to a loved one, would you regard them as *dead*, or merely tragically afflicted? For most of us, the latter attitude seems right. But if we can lose all our memories and still survive, Locke's account of what makes for personal survival must be mistaken.

There is also a less obvious difficulty. Under closer scrutiny Locke's account starts to look dangerously question-begging. We want to know what our identity over time involves and requires, and Locke has an answer: memory. But what is memory? The obvious answer (roughly) is: the ability to recall an incident or experience in one's own earlier life. Note the 'in one's own earlier life' clause. You can't remember undergoing another person's experiences; the only experiences you can remember – from the inside, from the perspective of the person who had them – are your own experiences. Memory thus *presupposes* personal identity. And if memory does presuppose personal identity, it cannot also be used to explain it informatively.

The Neo-Lockeans

We now zoom forward 300 or so years. The contemporary philosophers who follow Locke (the 'Neo-Lockeans'), such as Derek Parfit and Sydney Shoemaker, have made several moves to solve these problems.

The first is to broaden the range of psychological states that their account draws upon. It may seem clear enough that ordinary amnesia – the loss of all personal memories – is not fatal, but it is different in the case of a complete mind-zap (to use Shoemaker's term). If a device were placed over your head and obliterated all traces of your memories, and also your factual beliefs, your ambitions and intentions, your likes and dislikes, your values, your sexual orientation, your personality traits, your moral and aesthetic preferences, your linguistic abilities – everything that is distinctive about you in a psychological way – then it is far from clear that *you* would still exist. Given this, we can improve on Locke by incorporating into our account a much broader range of psychological states and traits. Instead of 'sameness of consciousness', the modern Neo-Lockeans talk in terms of 'sameness of psychology'. A person's psychology consists of memories, but also beliefs, values, character traits, preferences, intentions, hopes, and so forth. Since our psychological systems are many-stranded, even if your memories of your prior experiences are lost, much else that is distinctive about you in a mental way can remain, and, provided they do, you survive.

As we grow older our bodies change a good deal, but so too do our minds – and perhaps to a more dramatic extent. A psychology-based account of personal identity has to be able to accommodate psychological change. The account of Shoemaker and Parfit does so. In the now-standard Neo-Lockean terminology, a single persisting psychological state – such as your memory of what happened on your first day at school, or your belief that $2 + 2 = 4$, or your love of Baroque chamber music – is known as a 'psychological connection'. It may be that there is no one psychological connection that runs through the whole length of an average person's life. But this does not matter. We can say that an earlier and a later person are *psychologically continuous* if they are joined by a chain of overlapping psychological connections. Since psychological change is (usually) fairly gradual, from day to day our psychologies overlap to a high degree. The final step is to hold that it is psychological continuity, thus understood, which makes for personal identity. Or, more formally:

A person P_1 at t_1 is numerically identical with a person P_2 at t_2 if, and only if, they are linked by the relationship of psychological continuity.

The absence of psychological connections linking (say) the earliest and latest phases of a particular person's life is now no obstacle to these phases belonging to the same person. Provided that the early and late phases are linked by an overlapping series of psychological connections, they are psychologically continuous, and this is enough to render them phases of a single person's life.[7]

Causation: the essential (self-preserving) cement

Thus just one difficulty remains. We need a way of specifying the conditions under which a memory – or any other sort of psychological state – persists through time which does not presuppose anything about personal identity. The Neo-Lockeans have a solution to this problem too.

Suppose that an exact replica of you as you currently are comes into existence a few miles away – or in Australia, or on a distant (but hospitable) planet, it matters not. According to quantum theory such things *can* happen. It is possible for complex objects to just pop into existence, as spontaneous products of the quantum fields which pervade space – it's just that such events are highly improbable. So let's suppose the highly improbable has happened. Since your newly created replica is an exact duplicate of you, he or she will be exactly similar to you in all psychological respects as well. Hence you will both have exactly the same personal memories, factual beliefs, character traits, values, intentions, hopes, fears – the lot. Of course this similarity won't last long. When your replica starts having experiences which you don't, their memories will diverge from yours. But let's focus on the moment your replica comes into existence.

Does this mean your replica *really* remembers the experiences you had on your first day of school? Of course not: the replica only seems to remember these experiences, whereas you really do. According to the Neo-Lockeans, your memories are genuine by virtue of being *causally dependent* on your earlier experiences. If your first day at school had gone very differently than it did, your experiences on that day would have been different, and your memories correspondingly different. Your replica's memories are *not* causally linked to your earlier experiences, and this is why they are illusory. The same holds for other sorts of psychological connections. If your parents had emigrated and raised you in a different country (for example), your life would have gone very differently, and your current psychology would be very different – your replica's would be just the same. Your current psychology, in all its various aspects, is causally dependent on the psychological states you had in the past, whereas your replica's is not.

It is by appealing in this way to relationships of causal dependency that the Neo-Lockean can fill the gap in Locke's own account of personal identity: they are able to distinguish real from counterfeit memories, and, more generally, real from counterfeit psychological connections. If psychological connections require causal dependencies across time, so too does the relationship which (according to the Neo-Lockeans) secures personal identity itself: psychological *continuity* – given that this relationship is made up of overlapping psychological connections.

Let's return to the teleportation station. You have entered the cubicle, and have spent the last few minutes deliberating whether you should press the button – you haven't travelled by this method before, and (naturally) you are a little anxious. If you do press the button, you will lose consciousness, and your body and brain will both be annihilated, but only after having been subjected to a detailed scan; a short while later, a replica of you will be created on Mars, using the data from this scan. You aren't worried about the annihilation of your body; you are confident that this will be quick and painless. What you are worried about is the identity of the person who will emerge from the teleportation chamber on Mars. Will that person be *you*, or a mere replica of you?

If you believe that you are a human organism and nothing more, and that sameness of person consists of sameness of organism, then if you want to survive you shouldn't press the button. The person who emerges from the teleportation chamber will most definitely not be you. As we saw earlier, an animal does *not* survive physical obliteration.

But if you have been persuaded by Locke that it is mental continuity that makes for personal identity through time, even if this continuity is sustained by a succession of different material substances, you should be at least open to the possibility that the person who emerges from the chamber on Mars will be you. Moreover, if you find it plausible to think that the identity-preserving mental continuity is *psychological continuity*, then there is every reason to believe that this relationship can be preserved through teleportation. After all, the person who emerges from the chamber on Mars will be an exact psychological duplicate of you, and – critically – each and every one of their psychological states will directly causally depend on your current psychological states. If the Neo-Lockean account of personal identity is correct, there is every reason to be confident that teleportation is person-preserving.

Transportation at light-speed, without any risk to your self, would then become a possibility, at least in principle. So too would moving from one body to another body. If mind-transfer devices become available, then body-swaps would also be possible. And Locke's dream of liberating the self from its bodily confinement will have been realized.

4. The Phenomenal and the Psychological

Locke's claim that mental continuity is the key to understanding our persistence through time seems compelling – I for one have always found it so. Provided our mental lives continue without interruption, it seems hard to believe we ourselves could cease to exist. However, to be in a position to assess the merits of Locke's approach to the self we need a clear understanding of the *nature* of mental continuity. What, precisely, does it involve?

According to most contemporary defenders of Locke, as we saw in the previous chapter, the self-sustaining form of mental continuity is *psychological* in character. A person who exists tomorrow – or next week, or next year – will be *me* if they have my memories and personality. Since this person will be very similar to me psychologically, and, moreover, *believe* that they are me, it certainly seems as though this person has a reasonable claim on *being* me.

But is the psychological theory the best that the Lockean approach can deliver? Or can the notion that our lives are measured by mental continuity be developed in a different way? The answer, I think, is a resounding and unqualified 'yes'.

Ultimate games machines

Increasing numbers of people spend sizeable amounts of their time playing video games, and the technology has developed a long way in a short time. In the early days of computer gaming, a tennis game consisted of a white dot moving back and forth across a black screen, with two vertical white lines moving up and down acting as rackets. A game of tennis for the current generation of machines resembles a video recording of a *real* tennis match, featuring players based on real athletes operating in three dimensions. Where is this development heading? Will there be an *ultimate* games machine in the future?

If so, this ultimate machine would be capable of providing a complete simulation, one which embraces all aspects of experience. It wouldn't just supply sound and vision, but also a full range of fully realistic bodily experiences. Thus if you are playing tennis you will *feel yourself* running across the court as your arm swings the racket and hits the ball, and similarly for all the other activities you choose to perform.

The average lounge isn't big enough for you to actually run about over the equivalent of a whole tennis court – let alone contain the entire mountain you could choose to ski down, or a battlefield extending over many miles – but, with the ideal gaming machine, this wouldn't matter: all your experiences would be generated by the helmet you would (probably) be wearing, which would act directly on your brain. Thanks to this device, you could have the fully realistic experience of exploring any environment you choose without leaving your armchair.

There is a second reason why current gaming machines are limited: they provide a simulation of your external environment, but they leave *you* unchanged. You may be able to find out how well you would cope (say) driving in a Formula 1 race against the current crop of championship drivers. But what if you want to experience what it's like to *be* a champion driver yourself, and to have *their* reflexes and driving know-how? The same applies for other simulations: aren't we curious to know what it feels like to *be* a tennis player – or snowboarder, or footballer – at the top of their game? Or a general commanding divisions of troops over the course of a great battle?

To cater to these desires, the ultimate games machine will need to have the ability to alter one's *mind* just as easily and comprehensively as it can alter the external appearance of one's body. If you want to know what it was like for Napoleon to be commanding his troops at the Battle of Waterloo – what it was like *on the inside*, for Napoleon himself – then the machine will provide you with a working replica of Napoleon's psychology. The machine would temporarily remove (and store) your psychology – your memories, beliefs, ambitions and intentions, hopes and fears, linguistic and intellectual capacities – and replace them with copies of the French general's. And with this accomplished, the game can begin.

Our ideal gaming device is so powerful that a more impressive-sounding name is surely appropriate, so let's call it the Ultimate Simulation Machine, or the U-SIM for short. Since Napoleon has been dead for nearly 200 years, even a device with these impressive capabilities would only be able to offer an approximation of Napoleon's mind, based on histories of his life, autobiographies, and so forth. But it would be otherwise with contemporary people. If the technology for the U-SIM becomes available in the future, we can suppose that the technology needed to non-invasively 'read' and accurately replicate a person's psychology, down to the last detail, will also exist. In which case, you really will be able to know what it is like to be someone else.

Could the U-SIM be built? Like teleportation devices, it would require technology far beyond anything we currently possess. But as we saw in connection with teleportation, technology is advancing very quickly: the beginnings of neural interface technology already exist. Rapid progress is being made on chip implants, with some of the technology already reaching the market. It's already possible to buy an Emotiv 'EPOC' headset – a 'high resolution, neuro-signal acquisition and processing wireless neuroheadset' – for computer gaming, for as little as $300.[8] Who knows what the next few decades will bring?

A virtual adventure

In his influential work on personal identity, Locke tried to devise a theory that allows us to survive all the sorts of changes and transformations that we can easily envisage ourselves surviving. One of his key insights was that if your current body were to be destroyed, but your mental life gets transferred to a new body, then there are compelling reasons for supposing that *you* would be transferred to this new body as well. But, as we saw in the previous chapter, Locke's own memory-based theory faces problems, which the currently popular psychological continuity theory was designed to solve. However, as we shall now see, the psychological continuity theory *also* faces problems of a profound sort – problems created by the possibilities opened up by the U-SIM.

Let's suppose that you have decided to spend a bit of time in the Napoleon-at-Waterloo battle simulation. You put on the headset and activate the U-SIM. The changes come thick and fast. You don't just see the battle, you start to hear and smell it, and before long your bodily sensations also fall into line. You are on horseback; soon, you *feel* the horse beneath you. Your *thoughts* take on a Gallic colouring: you think 'As I've often said, *he who fears being conquered is certain of defeat*. Never has this been more true!', but in French, not English. Since your psychology is now a reconstruction of Napoleon's, this switch of language does not feel strange. When you recall episodes of your past life, they are events in Napoleon's life that you remember. Of your own original psychology, not a trace remains. But since you now believe that you are Napoleon – and have never been anyone else – you are oblivious to this fact.

A few hours later, the U-SIM does what you programmed it to do and brings the adventure to a close; your visual field shimmers and swirls, you feel a few moments of confusion, and you find yourself returned to your own body, in your familiar living room, with your own mind, but with one addition: you can now remember what it was like to be Napoleon at the crucial battle. After mentally reviewing your most recent vivid adventure, you decide it was well worth making the trip.

Streams of life

Now, in describing this scenario I have assumed that *you* are present throughout. The U-SIM produces a massive quantity of psychological disruption, but it does not cause you to lose consciousness: you remain fully awake and aware throughout the transition. You continue to have visual, auditory and bodily sensations – recall the swirl and shimmer in your visual field – and you remain aware of your (changing) environment. You continue to feel emotions, and you also continue to *think* throughout the whole episode, albeit in a more disjointed and confused way than usual (but not to an unprecedented or impossible extent: anyone who is bilingual will have had the experience of thinking successive thoughts in different languages). Given that you remain continuously conscious throughout, isn't it obvious that you continue to exist, that you continue to be *you* throughout?

The problem from the vantage point of the Neo-Lockean approach is that, if this account of personal identity is correct, you simply *can't* survive this U-SIM adventure. For the Neo-Lockean, the continued existence of a person depends entirely on psychological connections, or individual psychological states, such as memories, beliefs, intentions and the like. When the U-SIM replaces your psychological system with a duplicate of Napoleon's, you lose *all* your original psychological states within just a few seconds, and there are *no* psychological connections whatsoever linking the person who exists prior to the transformation and the person who exists after it. As a consequence, if the psychological account were true, you would cease to exist when your virtual adventure begins. But this is implausible in the extreme: if your stream of consciousness continues to flow, you continue to exist. The notion that you could cease to exist while continuing to experience normally is simply absurd. Since the psychological account delivers the result that you *do* cease to exist, it looks as though this account cannot be true.

This scenario points to one conclusion: provided our streams of consciousness continue to flow without interruption we will continue to exist, irrespective of what changes take place. What the U-SIM makes clear is that when it comes to our continued existence, it is *experiential continuity*, not psychological continuity – as the Neo-Lockeans would have it – that is of paramount importance.

Experiential continuity is simply the continuity we find in our ordinary conscious experience, from moment to moment. Think of what it is like to hear a sound droning on, or watch a bird flying across the sky, or your own hand moving across your field of vision as you slowly wave it back and forth, or feel the water running across your skin as you take a shower. This is the stuff of the sensory forms of experiential continuity, but our inner conscious thinking is similarly continuous, as one thought unfolds before flowing into the next. It is not for nothing that psychologists talk of 'streams of consciousness'. For like a stream of water, our consciousness *as a whole* exhibits continuous flow in all its parts. And, as our example suggests, even the most radical of mental transformations – borrowing the psychology of a French army commander – do not threaten our survival, provided that continuity in *consciousness* is not interrupted.

So as to have a convenient way of referring to this last claim, let's call it the *Continuous Consciousness Thesis*, which we can abbreviate to just 'C-thesis'. More formally:

C-thesis: *for as long as one's consciousness continues to flow without interruption, one continues to exist, irrespective of any other changes one undergoes.*

The C-thesis has a good deal of plausibility, and, as we shall shortly see, its implications are radical.

Beyond personhood

Locke held that our identity was not tied to any one substance, and accepting the C-thesis leads to the same conclusion. If your current stream of consciousness were sustained by a succession of different physical systems, e.g. if it is moved from body to body, from brain to brain, it would not matter: provided your consciousness flows on without interruption, you will go on existing.

So far, so Lockean. But no further. Recall another of Locke's doctrines: the claim that we are *persons*, i.e. beings that have consciousness and self-consciousness, and are distinguished by their rationality and intelligence, their ability to 'conceive of themselves as themselves' persisting through time. Locke's concept of a person is an important one, and it certainly applies to all of us *some* of the time. But does it necessarily apply to all of us *all* of the time? Arguably not. There are circumstances in which it looks very much as though *we* exist even though we lack the requisite level of cognitive sophistication to satisfy Locke's definition. It is for this reason that very young infants are not Lockean persons, and likewise many brain-damaged adults. Our C-thesis allows subjects with comparatively primitive cognitive powers to persist through time – provided their consciousness continues, in some form or other. Since it is likely that young children and (many) brain-damaged adults *do* have streams of consciousness, an experience-based account of our persistence conditions embraces a wider range of subjects, in a wider range of conditions, than the psychological account. For this reason alone such an account is more plausible than Locke's.[9]

In fact, the experience-based approach is compatible with us being able to survive transformations that would take us still further away from personhood. In the U-SIM scenario, the psychological changes you underwent were in one respect not very radical. Yes, you ended up with a completely new psychology, but it was still a *human* psychology – that of Napoleon. There is no reason why this should always be the case. If the technology were to exist for U-SIMs, we might know so much about the brains of various animal species that we can both replicate their psychological systems and simulate the sorts of experiences they have. In which case, for your next U-SIM session, instead of opting to find out what it's like to be a human general during a famous battle, you might choose to find out what it's like to be a tiger on a jungle hunt, a bat exploring its cave, or an eagle gliding over the Alps – the possibilities are endless. The key point is that provided when you embark on your virtual reality trip you remain fully conscious throughout the transition – you continue to have *some* visual, auditory and bodily sensations, along with emotional feelings – then there's no doubt that it's *you* who gets to enjoy the ride.

A paradox resolved

In a much-discussed paper, 'The Self and the Future', published in 1970, the English philosopher Bernard Williams sought to cast doubt on the entire Lockean approach to the self in a novel way. Williams' argument hinges on our different responses to a pair of imaginary cases. The following two scenarios are in some respects simpler than those deployed by Williams, but the essential ingredients are the same.[10]

Scenario 1 *Your long and hitherto successful criminal career has come to an end: you have finally been apprehended by the authorities,* *who are keen to question you about your past deeds. Alas, the authorities in question prefer to use an old-fashioned method of interrogation: physical torture – brutal but effective. After your capture your interrogators inform you that to avoid leaving incriminating traces on your own body, your mind will be relocated into a different body. The torture will then be carried out, and you will be returned to your original (unblemished) body after you have confessed. Thanks to recent advances in neuroscience, the body-swap will not require a brain transplant: a 'psy-state transfer' machine will be used instead. This ingenious device is able to copy the psychological states (memories, beliefs, intentions, personality traits, and so on) from one brain to another brain, without any recourse to surgery. A helmet is placed over your head, and the transfer machine activated. You wake up a little nauseous, and clearly in a different body, but feel much like your usual self. You dread what lies ahead. Your fears turn out to be justified: the torture, when it comes, is as terrible as you expected.*

In the second scenario, a similar psy-transfer device is put to use, but in a slightly different way:

Scenario 2 *Your long and hitherto successful criminal career is almost over. You will soon be arrested, and you are under no illusions as to the treatment you can expect to receive when apprehended: dreadful physical torture. But your accomplices tell that they have worked out a way for you to avoid this fate. They have managed to obtain a 'psy-state transfer' machine, and will use it to transfer your psychology into a storage device, while copying the psychology of someone else – someone wholly ignorant of your doings – into your brain. While grateful for your collaborators' efforts on your behalf, you are not in the least comforted by what they are proposing. Possessing* *different memories and beliefs will scarcely stop you from feeling the pain when your body is being tortured. At most, when your original psychology is restored, you will not be able to remember the torture, but this will do nothing to make the pain any less agonizing while it is being inflicted. If you do what your accomplices want, it seems you will suffer a double indignity: you will not only be tortured, you will be brainwashed into believing you are someone as well.*

If we confine our attention to what happens to *you*, both scenarios involve a device that shifts your psychological states from your original brain to a different location. What makes the cases intriguing is that what look to be similar sets of facts can be interpreted very differently.

When reading the first scenario, most people agree that it sounds plausible that you have been moved from your original body to a different body, the body that receives the terrible torture. In the second scenario, when considering what your collaborators are telling you, the notion that the psy-state transfer device will successfully relocate you into a different body does not ring true. Yet both scenarios involve precisely the same form of mental transfer. How does this shift in the narrative have such an impact on who ends up experiencing the agonizing torture?[11]

Faced with this predicament some philosophers have argued that what these scenarios really illustrate is that we can't hope to learn anything about the kind of thing we are by far-fetched fantasies or sci-fi tales. Williams himself suggests that our ability to make sense of the second scenario implies that we believe, deep down, that we are fundamentally our bodies, or human organisms. It is because we do believe this that we can make sense of the idea that we could survive vast amounts of psychological disruption and manipulation, and still have the capacity to feel pain if our bodies are tortured. But, as Williams is well aware, the fact that so many of us can easily imagine circumstances in which we and our bodies go their separate ways does not sit easily with the claim that we also believe that we and our bodies are identical.

We are now in a position to see that there is a different – better – diagnosis of the puzzle. As the U-SIM scenarios demonstrate, mental continuity has two distinguishable elements: *experiential* continuity and *psychological* continuity. Experiential continuity exists within our streams of consciousness, and consists of the felt flow of experience from moment to moment. Psychological continuity is based on causal dependencies between earlier and later psychological states. These same U-SIM scenarios also suggest that our continued survival and experiential continuity are very closely bound together: provided we continue to have experiences, we will continue to exist, irrespective of what other changes may take place.

Now, in the thought experiments Williams outlines, no mention whatsoever is made of experiential continuity; all the talk is of *psychological* states and transfers. Given this, and given the importance of experiential continuity to our continued existence, it is not surprising that what is really going on – what is really happening to *us* – is so unclear. Indeed, if it is experiential continuity which really matters – as I have been arguing – the fact that Williams' scenarios make no mention of it *should* leave us unclear as to our fate.

The following two variants of the second scenario should make the point. Here's the first:

Scenario 2* *You are on the verge of being captured, and excruciating torture will swiftly follow. Your well-meaning collaborators say they have a solution to your problem: they have managed to get their hands on a psy-state transfer device, which will allow them to exchange your psychology with that of somebody else — someone who is entirely ignorant of all your doings, but who richly deserves to be punished. Your spirits are lifted, and you ask for clarification as to how the device functions. Your collaborators do not know all the details, but they do know that the device does not relocate streams of consciousness — it only affects psychological states such as memories, personality traits and the like — and that, for it to function, both subjects must be fully awake and aware throughout. However, they tell you not to worry: all the evidence suggests that the mental transfer is quite painless, with most subjects feeling nothing worse than a little disorientation.*

We now know exactly what would happen to your stream of consciousness if the psy-state transfer device were to be used: nothing at all. And from a purely self-interested perspective, the news is not good. Since your original stream of consciousness remains with your original body throughout, it seems clear that any pain that is inflicted on that body will be felt by you, and you alone. Thanks to the psy-state transfer, you will (in effect) believe that you are someone else, and have this person's memories. But as we all know, having delusory beliefs about one's past does not, in and of itself, prevent one from feeling pain.

Now consider the following:

Scenario 2** *You are about to be captured and tortured, but your collaborators tell you not to worry. They have got their hands on a total mental transfer device, and before the torture begins both your psychology and your stream of consciousness will be transferred into a different body. What's more, the transfer process does not produce any loss of consciousness – you will remain fully awake and aware throughout. You are not in the least consoled by this prospect. How could having your own consciousness and psychology shifted into a different body possibly prevent you feeling the pain that is inflicted on your original body?*

Your negative response to this option definitely does not ring true: your failure to be consoled now seems unjustified. If your mind *in its entirety* – both your consciousness and psychology – is shifted to a new body, then it is clear that *you* also come to inhabit this new body, and so would not be in a position to feel any pain that will later be inflicted on your original body.

I suggested earlier that the original Williams scenarios are ambiguous because they fail to provide us with any information about experiential continuity: we are left guessing at the fate of the subject's streams of consciousness. But when the facts about experiential continuity *are* supplied, the fates of the subjects in question become clear. This result provides powerful additional evidence that, when it comes to our continued existence, it is experiential rather than psychological continuity which matters. The next step is to fashion an account of the nature of the self that exploits this finding as fully as possible.

5. Selves, Powers and Subjects

When I began my own investigations into the nature of the self it was not very long before I was led to the point we have now reached. Locke's claim that our continued existence is tied to mental continuity, rather than any particular body, struck me as very compelling. But I found the then-standard way of developing this insight – the psychological view – a good deal less appealing. It wasn't long before I became convinced, in large part by the sort of considerations we met in the previous chapter, that an experience- or consciousness-based approach to the self made the most sense.

But I then hit the philosophical equivalent of a wall. When I turned to extant experience-based accounts of the self, for one reason or another, I found them unconvincing. So I found myself forced to construct a theory of my own. The theory I eventually settled on, and the rationale underlying it, will be outlined over the course of this chapter.

The conception of the self to which I was led is in some respects a very radical one: if I am right, we are not like any other kind of thing at all. Most of us think we have potential – even if we aren't always making the most of what we have. According to my account of the self, there is a very real sense in which we are *nothing but* potential.

Subjects versus persons

We have so far uncovered one vital clue to our fundamental nature: provided our streams of consciousness continue to flow – provided we continue to experience continuously, without interruption – we continue to exist, irrespective of what other changes might befall us. If this is all that it takes for our selves to persist, what sort of thing can we be?

We know this much at least: we are the *kind of thing which is able to be conscious*. And there is a name for such things: *subjects of experience*. You are a subject of experience, so am I, so too are all normally functioning human beings who have ever lived, and so too are dogs, cats and rats, and any sentient machines or alien life-forms that are out there in the rest of the Universe.

From this perspective, Locke was wrong to hold that biographical memory – or more generally, psychological continuity – makes for sameness of self over time, but he wasn't necessarily wrong in claiming that there is a high level concept which applies both to us and to all those non-human entities which have minds and streams of consciousness of their own. For we clearly *do* belong to the class of things that enjoy (and suffer) experiences. And this ability to experience is an essential property of beings such as ourselves; if we lose it, irretrievably, we cease to be.

For what it's worth, the doctrine that we are fundamentally subjects of experience has a long history. Platonic souls and Cartesian selves both count as subjects of experience, and the many religious traditions that believe in reincarnation (found in just about every part of the world at some period in history) are committed to the same view. Since reincarnated souls often remember nothing of their past lives, these souls can survive rapid and complete psychological transformations.

The essence of self

The view that we are subjects of experience (or, simply, *subjects*) may be pervasive in human history, but it has not found favour among many contemporary philosophers. This is because they tend to equate subjects with *immaterial selves*, of the kind defended by Descartes, which these days are widely viewed as problematic.

One of the reasons for this is as simple as it is surprising: Descartes' selves don't sleep, not any of them. Ever. Why? Because if we follow Descartes and take being conscious to be an essential property of selves, then, since a thing cannot lose its essential properties and continue to exist, selves cannot *lose consciousness* and continue to exist. Any self that ceases to be conscious ceases to exist. If we fall into dreamless sleep as often as we seem to, as often as science has shown us to do (i.e. most nights), then our lives are much shorter than most of us believe: we will all perish whenever we next fall unconscious!

An alternative way of thinking of subjects was suggested by Locke. As it happens, Locke was well aware of

Descartes' stance on the issue of sleeping souls, writing in Book II of his *Essay Concerning Human Understanding*: 'I know it is an opinion, that the soul always thinks, and that it has the actual perception of ideas in itself constantly' (2.1.9). However, he goes on to mock it: 'I confess myself to have one of those dull souls, that doth not perceive itself always to contemplate ideas; nor can conceive it any more necessary for the soul always to think, than for the body always to move.' Locke continues:

> [having experiences is] to the soul what motion is to the body; not its essence, but one of its operations. And therefore, though thinking be supposed never so much the proper action of the soul, yet it is not necessary to suppose that it should be always thinking, always in action ... We know certainly, by experience, that we sometimes think; and thence draw this infallible consequence, that there is something in us that has a power to think. (2.1.10)

Locke is suggesting that while enjoying conscious experience is something souls can do, it doesn't mean they must always do so. A car has the capacity to move itself; but this capacity can exist without always being exercised. Similarly, your TV may not at this very moment be displaying images, but it has the ability to do so.

What Locke is proposing – although he fails to elaborate on the idea – is that the relationship between souls and actual experience is analogous to these cases. That we sometimes have experiences is beyond question. But the only thing we can conclude from this is that there is 'something in us that has a power to enjoy experiences' – or, more generally, that we have the capacity to be conscious. Since this capacity can exist when it is not being exercised, it is possible for us to survive periods of unconsciousness. Provided we retain the *capacity* to be conscious, we continue to exist, even if this capacity remains dormant.

Taking the essence of subjects to be the capacity to be conscious offers a solution to the problem of how we can survive periods of unconsciousness, and it also provides us with a way of answering the 'What are we?' question. We are things with a very distinctive feature, namely the capacity to be conscious.

Some conceptual engineering

This is a promising start, but we haven't quite arrived at our destination.

How precisely should we think of these *things* that we are? What is the relationship between subjects and the objects of other kinds – such as brains, or souls – which possess these capacities?

If the capacity to have conscious experiences is in itself sufficient to make anything a subject (and hence a self), then we can define what a subject is entirely in terms of this very property. Accordingly, let's use the neutral term *Consciousness-system*, or *C-system*, to refer to things – irrespective of their other features – which possess the capacity to produce or enjoy conscious stream-like experience.

Healthy human brains have the ability to be conscious, so they incorporate C-systems, but so do the brains of dolphins and dogs – not to mention vampire brains and sentient computers (assuming for illustrative purposes that these exist). Of course, when it comes to their physical makeup, the brains of humans and vampires are very different – and sentient computers even more so by virtue of being non-biological. Objects of very different kinds *can* possess C-systems, provided they possess capacities for consciousness.

I have been talking of C-systems as 'things' which possess capacities for unified streams of consciousness, but haven't yet said precisely how we should think of them. Having come this far there is a very natural (almost inevitable) way to proceed. We can abstract away from the differences between biological and non-biological subjects, and isolate the factor that is most relevant so far as subject-hood is concerned, by taking a C-system to *consist* of capacities for experience, and nothing more. A C-system on this view – one I will henceforth adopt – is a continuous (or uninterrupted) capacity for experience. C-systems, and so subjects, exist for as long as they retain their capacity for consciousness, but no longer.

By taking this step we exclude from subjects everything that is not essential to their existence, and establish them as a distinct kind of thing in their own right.

Even if capacities for experience will usually belong to some or other ordinary object of a more familiar kind – e.g. a biological brain, an immaterial substance or a sentient computer chip – it remains the case that C-systems are distinct from these objects, by virtue of consisting of only a subset of the properties these other objects possess. A healthy human brain, for example, has capacities for experience, but it has many other properties as well: it weighs about three pounds and contains billions of neurons and glial cells, along with several miles of blood vessels and the blood they carry.

Selves and potentials

The notion that *we* are nothing more than a continuous potential for experience may sound downright bizarre initially, but, as we have just seen, there is a clear rationale for it. Moreover, there is nothing suspect or dubious about the notion of an uninterrupted *potential*. A Maglev train-track is a useful illustration of this point. Maglev trains run on powerful magnetic fields generated by their tracks. These fields propel the train forward, but they also levitate the train, ensuring a significantly smoother ride than is possible on trains that are in physical contact with their tracks.

Despite its complexity, a Maglev track is quite simple in one respect: it generates a single, continuous magnetic field throughout its entire length, irrespective of whether a train is present. This magnetic potential (or capacity) is not directly perceivable – you can't see the magnetic field itself – but it is nonetheless *there*, as a real property of the track, as real as any other (such as its mass or length). If you were to move your compass close to the track it would go haywire.

What I am proposing is that a subject of experience is also a single uninterrupted potential. But whereas the potential running along the length of a Maglev track extends across space, the potential that constitutes a persisting subject extends across time and, when activated, produces experiences (of one kind or another) rather than motion.[12]

This last fact is crucial: it is because C-systems can produce *experiences* that they are candidates for being selves. The experiences you have been having since you woke up this morning, like all the experiences you have ever had, have been generated by the triggering of the various experiential capacities you possess, or, in other words, by your C-system. Provided your current C-system continues to exist, your capacity to enjoy rich and varied streams of consciousness will also continue to exist, and so will you.

Capacity allocation: the C-solution

Tomorrow, there will be billions of subjects in existence – and next week, and next year – all of whom possess capacities for experience. We need a way of deciding which of these future capacities belong to me and which belong to you (or some other subject). Can we answer this question without appealing to persisting objects such as brains or souls? Can an answer to the question remove any doubt whatsoever that the future subjects that say they are me really are *me*?

Yes, we can. If we know anything about subjects, it is that experiences in a single stream of consciousness all belong to the same subject, irrespective of any changes or transformations the subject undergoes. If the *experiences* in a single stream of consciousness necessarily belong to the same subject, so too do the *capacities* for experience which are producing this stream. Capacities which are able to contribute experiences to unified streams of consciousness can't fail to belong to a single self. This is why, when introducing the notion of a C-system, I stipulated that in order to qualify as a C-system a collection of capacities for experience have to be capable of producing unified streams of consciousness.

We now have a new account of what subjects are – experiential potentials – and the beginnings, at least, of an account of what the persistence of subjects involves. Bringing these together delivers the following picture of what you are. It takes a little unpacking, but the underlying message is clear and simple.

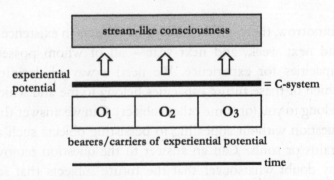

The self: the basic picture

The rectangle at the top of the figure represents the unified stream-like consciousness that your C-system – depicted by the central line – can produce. This continuous, uninterrupted experiential potential is what you fundamentally are, or so I am proposing. At any one time only a small number of our complete complement of experiential capacities will usually be active (if you look away from this page, capacities for visual experience which were previously dormant will be triggered), and when we are dreamlessly asleep none of our experiential capacities will be active. But what makes both active and inactive capacities belong to a single subject is the same ability: to contribute to unified streams of consciousness.

At the bottom of the diagram, the objects which possess these experiential capacities are depicted in the form of a series of rectangles, labelled O_1, O_2, and O_3. Over time, the objects which carry or sustain a subject's experiential potential can change – e.g. a subject may start off with a human brain, but end up with a vampire brain or silicon brain. Provided this base-level change doesn't destroy (or interrupt) the continuity of the experiential potential, the subject survives. In this particular case, the subject's experiential potential is grounded in O_1, then O_2 and finally O_3.

In reality, experiential potentials don't float free of the objects which possess them in the way shown. (It would be very odd if they did!) They are shown in this way to indicate as clearly as possible that selves-in-the-form-of-C-systems are distinct from the objects (such as brains) which happen to possess experiential capacities. Just like a magnetic field is distinct from – by virtue of being a property of – the hunk of metal that carries it.

Refinements

If a particular C-system has the ability to produce stream-like experiences (of one kind or another) *throughout* a given interval of time (an hour, say), its experience-producing ability can be said to be 'continuously operational' during that period. The C-systems of some real subjects may be continuously operational for the entire duration of their lives, e.g. they may live for 80 years, and have the ability to be conscious continuously throughout that interval. But we are not like that. Therefore we need to define our persistence in terms of capacities for consciousness that exist for briefer periods. You may not be able to be conscious for 80 years, but you can be continuously conscious for shorter periods, such as 12 hours, or 6 hours, or 6 minutes or 6 seconds. Talking in terms of 'temporally extended phases of continuously operational C-systems' is a bit of a mouthful, so let's abbreviate and call these collections of capacities *C-phases* instead.

Since the experiential capacities which belong to a C-phase all belong to a single subject – since they can all contribute to a single stream of consciousness – so too do the capacities which belong to *overlapping* C-phases. The kind of overlap I have in mind arises when earlier and later C-phases have a common part, as shown below.

Here there are two overlapping C-phases which share the experiential capacities labelled 'C2'. Streams A and B (indicated by the arrows) are the streams of consciousness which C-phase 1 and C-phase 2 can produce, respectively. Experiential capacities C_1 and C_2 can produce a single uninterrupted stream of consciousness which means they belong to the same subject. To keep things simple, let's suppose that subject is you. Since capacities C_2 and C_3 can also produce a single uninterrupted stream of consciousness, we know they too belong to a single subject; consequently, since C_2 belongs to you, so too will C_3. This mechanism for preserving the identity of subjects through overlapping C-phases can be extended indefinitely into the future. Let's use the term *C-continuous* to refer to experiential capacities which belong to a chain of partially overlapping C-phases.

A rope can have great strength even though there is no one fibre running through its entire length; the strength of the rope derives from the number and character of the individual fibres it is composed of, and the manner in which they overlap. In a similar fashion, there is no single C-phase which extends through the entire life of a

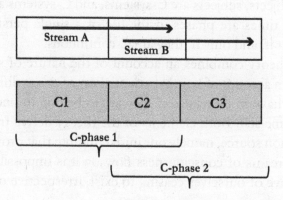

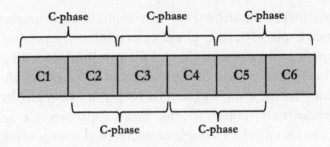

Experiential capacities that belong to a single C-phase can produce consciousness continuously, and so belong to one and the same subject. C-phases that are more widely separated in time, such as C1 and C6, but which overlap by sharing parts in the manner shown above, also belong to the same subject. Capacities linked in this way are *C-continuous*.

typical (human) subject. Nonetheless, series of overlapping C-phases are sufficient to maintain the existence of a single subject, as shown in the figure above.

In my other writings on the subject, I have referred to this way of looking at things as *C-theory*.[13] What the theory amounts to can be succinctly summarized thus: we are subjects, subjects are C-systems, and C-systems at different times are phases in the life of a single persisting subject if, and only if, they are C-continuous.

C-theory combines an account of the nature of selves with an account of how experiential capacities at different times have to be related if they are to belong to one and the same self. Both elements of the theory derive from a common source, namely our initial finding: that provided our streams of consciousness flow on it is impossible to conceive of ourselves ceasing to exist, irrespective of any changes we might undergo. Just as it is natural to think that you will continue to exist for as long as you continue to have experiences, so is it natural to think that you will continue to exist for as long as your *capacities* for experience continue to exist.

C-theory explains why, if, a few minutes from now, a perfect duplicate of you suddenly appears out of thin air, this person isn't you. They aren't you because they aren't connected to you as you now are by C-continuity, an uninterrupted experiential potential. Moreover, C-theory successfully liberates subjects of experience from objects of other kinds (such as brains or souls), by equating subjects with their only essential feature, the capacity to produce or enjoy experiences.

Selves as C-systems

The notion that we are fundamentally a collection of persisting capacities for experience doesn't correspond with how we are used to thinking of ourselves. But that does not mean it isn't true. Persisting potentials – of the sort which extend along Maglev tracks, say – are fully real parts of the real world, and the potentials in *our* case are for streams of consciousness, of the sort we are all enjoying from moment to moment, and which suffice to keep us in existence.

It is worth noting that C-theory is entirely neutral on the issue of whether or not consciousness is physical (here too it follows Locke). If experience is a physical phenomenon, entirely grounded in our physical brains, then our C-systems' capacities will also be grounded in our brains. If our experience is a non-physical phenomenon, a property of immaterial soul-substances in the way Descartes envisaged, then our C-systems will also be housed in these immaterial substances. Under either hypothesis, selves are the same kind of entity: they are beings with the potential for conscious experience.[14]

The fact that our core selves are C-systems does not mean that we lack *bodies*. It goes without saying that our minds are connected in all sorts of ways to our bodies, and it's because of these connections that we can interact with others, act on the world and perceive what's going on around us. Moreover, if our minds are grounded in neural activity in our brains (rather than in immaterial souls), then our capacities for consciousness are capacities that are present in, or possessed by, material things in the form of our brains. Accepting C-theory does not mean that in ordinary life we cannot continue to think of ourselves as embodied human beings in the usual sorts of ways – as beings who wear clothes, gain and lose weight, travel by train, and so forth. What it does bring is a commitment to a particular philosophical account of our relationship with our bodies.

If we take ourselves to be C-systems, then, although we *have* bodies, by virtue of being connected to one in various distinctive ways, we are not *numerically identical* with our bodies – i.e. we are not the same entities or objects as our bodies. There are two main reasons for this. First, a C-system consists of a collection of capacities for experience, and there is much more to a human body (and brain) than capacities of this sort. Second, there are circumstances in which our bodies and our C-systems could go their separate ways. If your brain were successfully transplanted into a new body, and your old body incinerated, since your brain carries your C-system, you would acquire a new body but you would not lose your self. And there are more radical ways in which our C-systems and our actual bodies could come apart. You might be reduced to *just* your brain (or even the parts which sustain consciousness) provided your neural tissues are supplied with blood and other nutrients so that they remain functional when removed from your body. Or the bite of a vampire might eliminate your current human body altogether by transforming it into a non-human body, while leaving you outwardly unchanged. Provided such transformations do not interfere with your capacity for consciousness, your self would survive.[15]

The self and the future

Of course vampire-induced bodily transformations exist only in fiction. But future technological developments may make equally radical bodily transformations possible.

So-called nano-machines are small enough to travel through one's blood stream and perform complex mechanical and chemical operations at the cellular level. Our current nano-technology is still in its infancy, but progress is rapidly being made, so in another fifty years

85

the following life-extension procedure might be routine. You have just, let's suppose, reached the age of twenty-five, the age at which neural decay typically sets in, and, like most of your friends and family, you decide to put a stop to it. You make an appointment at a local clinic, lie down on a bed and receive an injection of nano-machines. They get to work on your brain, replacing each neuron with a similarly sized silicon-based equivalent. Although at any one time only a tiny proportion of your brain cells are out of action, the machines work fast, and after a few hours you have a *completely new brain*, one that is entirely non-biological, one that will last you for centuries. Since you remain awake and fully conscious throughout the procedure, you evidently survive it. Yet you wouldn't and couldn't if your continued existence were tied to your original brain.

Not knowing what the future will bring does not prevent our now knowing what would and wouldn't be survivable. If we are C-systems, then we already know that *if* a future transformation radically changes our physical form but preserves our capacity for consciousness, then it is survivable; if it doesn't, then it isn't. If the procedure just outlined proves to be possible, since it does not interfere (or eliminate) one's capacity for consciousness, then by the lights of C-theory it is eminently survivable. By taking the capacity for consciousness to be our only essential property, C-theory allows us to survive transformations such as moving from body to body, or remaining within a body that is transformed from human to non-human. We can also survive the most radical *psychological* transformations, including trips into virtual realities equipped with radically different personalities.

Real and illusory selves

According to a famous line in the movie *The Usual Suspects* (which is a slightly misquoted line from the poet Baude- laire), 'The greatest trick the devil ever pulled was convincing the world that he doesn't exist.' Some philoso- phers and psychologists would say we are all victims of a similarly impressive trick: we are being deluded into thinking our selves exist, when in fact they don't. To make matters more complicated, *we* are the ones performing the trick.

While it may sound paradoxical, this claim lies at the heart of an influential trend in scientifically informed thinking about the self – one endorsed in two recent popular works: Julian Baggini's *The Ego Trick* (2011), and John Hood's *The Self Illusion* (2012). What its proponents maintain is that, thanks to discoveries in psychology, neuroscience and related disciplines, it is now looking very much as though we are powerfully disposed to be deluded as to our own real natures. As Baggini puts it: 'The Ego Trick is not to persuade us that we exist when we do not, but to make us believe that we are more sub- stantial and enduring than we really are. There may be an illusion as to *what* we really are, but not *that* we really are.' Hood takes a similar line, writing: 'We all certainly ex- perience some form of self but what we experience is a powerful deception generated by our brains for our own benefit.'

C-theory is supposed to be an account of the self, and hence our own real natures. Do these self-related scientific findings demonstrate that the conception of the self I have been defending here is just one more delusion? Not in the least.

The alleged 'self' delusion is complex, possessing as it does several interrelated aspects. One of the key delusions concerns the real nature of selves, and is broadly metaphysical in character. The main claim in this connection is that most of us are strongly inclined to believe that we are *atomic* selves, along the lines of Descartes' soul-substances, i.e. things that are essentially changeless, and thus capable of preserving our identity through time in an undiluted manner. Since in reality there are no such substances, save for elementary physical particles such as electrons, we are deluded as to our own natures. Or so the argument runs.

But C-theory does *not* claim that selves are atom-like or changeless. C-systems are not by their nature changeless, since a subject's experiential capacities can themselves change over time – anyone who has lost (or regained) their sight or hearing is an example of this. Nor need we suppose that the objects which possess our experiential capacities at any given time are themselves atomic in nature. This won't be the case if (as seems likely) our own experiential capacities reside in our brains, which are highly complex and constantly changing entities.

The second aspect of this ego trick consists of psychological (rather than metaphysical) delusions. These, it is argued, are systematic (mis)conceptions that many of us have about our own minds. There are several of these, and a large number of fascinating – and often surprising – empirical studies that are relevant to them.

We naturally assume that the bulk of our actions, and certainly all the important ones, are the product of our autonomous, conscious decision-making. In doing so, psychological and sociological surveys suggest that we tend to overlook the extent to which our actions are in fact conditioned by both social and genetic factors. Although we all know what it is like to consciously decide to do something, there is neuro-scientific evidence that our brains have often already selected our course of action *before* our conscious decision is made. We are also deluded about our autobiographical memories. Many of us naturally assume that memories are akin to video recordings, which gradually fade with age but remain essentially accurate (if blurred) records of our past experiences. Psychological research has shown that they are nothing of the kind. We remember far less of our lives than most of us suppose, and we remember very selectively, with events which conform to our (probably inaccurate) self-image being preferred. Our memories are not passive replays of (mental) recordings, but active re-creations, which typically involve a sizeable number of fictional elements.[16]

The research along these lines that Baggini and Hood summarize is certainly interesting, and potentially important in a number of respects. But what does it tell us about what we really are?

These results all go to suggest that our *psychological* selves, as we might call them, are less truly continuous – less solid – than we naturally assume. If you analyse personal persistence in terms of psychological continuity, which is made up of ingredients such as autobiographical memories, personality traits and the like, then these results undoubtedly compromise the solidity of the self. But the situation is very different if our continued existence depends entirely on experiential rather than psychological factors, as I have been arguing here. According to C-theory, a self remains in existence provided its capacity for conscious experience endures, irrespective of *any* and *all* psychological changes it might undergo. Since our identity – our existence – is entirely independent of both memory and personality, the findings *about* memory and personality outlined above do not automatically have any consequences for the way in which we persist through time. In fact, our capacity to enjoy continuous streams of conscious experience is unaffected by long-term variations in our character, or the accuracy (or inaccuracy) of our autobiographical memories, and it depends not at all on whether our decisions and actions are the products of our conscious decisions or some other factor(s).

Consequently, if we take ourselves to be subjects of experience, we are not deluding ourselves in the slightest if we also believe that we continue to exist, with our identity intact and undiluted, for decades on end. For we *do* persist in this way for as long as our capacity for consciousness is unimpaired. When it comes to self-delusions, not all selves are equal.

6. Taking the Plunge

Let's return to our main question: 'What am I? What are *you*?' A viable answer has to specify the kind of entity that we are. It also has to be able to supply a clear and convincing answer to a further question: 'How must I be related to someone who exists in the future if that someone is going to be *me*?' Motivated by the thought that we cannot fail to continue to exist provided our streams of consciousness continue to flow, C-theory equates us with subjects of experience, which are themselves composed of nothing more than capacities for experience. The theory also states that it is the ability to contribute to a single stream of consciousness that makes it possible for capacities for experience (both active and dormant) to belong to a single subject over intervals of time.

Streams of consciousness lie at the very heart of C-theory. If this account of the self is to have solid foundations it is crucial that streams of consciousness really do possess a genuine unity at and over time. For if they don't then we will lack *any* account of our persistence through time, let alone a convincing one. In this chapter we will be embarking on a new quest. We will be plunging into our streams of consciousness and trying to discover precisely what sort of unity they possess.

As our consciousness flows and changes, our experiences

at any given time, what we see, hear and feel is experienced together with the thoughts we think. The felt flow of experience from moment to moment is itself a distinctive form of unity, but one that holds *over* time, rather than *at* a time. How are these forms of unity best understood or explained?

These questions relating to the unity and structure of our everyday experience may seem quite abstract or obscure. But they are of foundational importance – much hangs on them, not least the viability of C-theory. Our consciousness is with us every moment of our waking lives; there is a very real sense in which nothing is closer to us, nothing is more familiar. Yet some of the most basic features of our consciousness are deeply puzzling, and there are competing and very different accounts of them. Moreover, one of these accounts brings with it a new conception of the self.

Unity

We'll start with the unity of consciousness *at* a time – we'll be turning to unity *over* time later. To bring this form of unity into clear focus it's worth carrying out a few simple exercises.

Start with what you can see, and take notice of the fact that the various contents in the right half of your field of vision are experienced together with all the contents in the left half.[17] This fact about your visual experience is so obvious that you may well have never paused to give it much thought. Even so, there's no denying that what you see to your left and what you see to your right *are* experienced together. Experiences that are experienced together in this way are called 'co-conscious'.

Now perform the same exercise with your sense of hearing. When you next hear two (or more) sounds at once, take note of the way that they too are co-conscious. Next, focus for a few seconds on some of your various bodily sensations – to keep things simple, we'll include any taste or smell sensations you may be enjoying in this category. Pay attention to how you can *feel* that your various limbs are arranged in a particular way – you don't need to look in order to know whether your arms are folded or not, or whether your legs are crossed. Also take notice of the sensations of pressure you can feel, on your feet or back. When you are confident that you are aware of the bulk of your bodily feelings, notice how these too are all experienced together, as part of a single unified conscious field, e.g. how the sensations of pressure on your back are co-conscious with (say) the minty-sensation on your tongue, and the latter are both co-conscious with your mild headache. Just as your visual and auditory sense-fields form unified ensembles, so too does your bodily sense-field.

Next into the mix are your conscious thoughts – the contents of your inner soliloquy – along with any mental images that may be running through your mind. If you are like most people, these will seem to occur somewhere behind your eyes and between your ears. The final step is to start paying attention to how these various different sorts of experience are themselves *all co-conscious with one another.* Your thoughts are co-conscious with your bodily sensations. Your thoughts and bodily sensations are co-conscious with your auditory experiences, and your auditory experiences are co-conscious with your visual experiences. Put another way, *every* part of your experience at any one time is co-conscious with every other part – and hence, all parts of your experience belong to a deeply unified conscious field.

Given that our consciousness *is* unified in this deep and distinctive way, what can be said about it? How should we understand this form of unity? Since the relationship between consciousness and the brain remains largely mysterious, we cannot hope for much illumination on that front, though insights may come as neuroscience advances. But perhaps there is something to be said about what the unity of consciousness involves at the purely experiential level. Is there anything *in* our experience that helps us to better understand experiential unity?

Enter the Ego

Think again of the various different types of experience you are having at the moment. It seems true to say that you are *aware* of everything that you are experiencing. You are aware of what you are seeing – the page in front of you, the surrounding room – you are also aware of your bodily sensations, your conscious thoughts, the sound of a distant car's horn, your overall mood. Since you are not (usually) paying equal attention to all the experiences that go to make up your consciousness at a given time, you are not aware of them in the same way, but you have *some* awareness of them, even if it is of a peripheral kind. An experience that you have no awareness of at all would not be a part of your consciousness.

This simple fact means that your awareness of what you are seeing and your awareness of what you are hearing aren't distinct; likewise for your awareness of your bodily sensations and auditory experiences. There's just *one* awareness, which takes in all the diverse parts and aspects of your current consciousness. Might it not be that all the contents of your consciousness are unified *because* they fall within the scope of a single awareness?

If this account of the unity of consciousness is correct – if there *is* a single awareness which is unifying your experience at every moment – then a typical episode of experiencing something has a bi-polar structure, as depicted below.

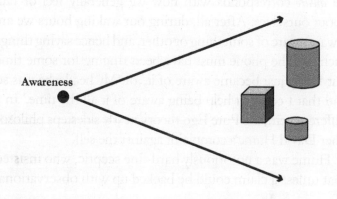

On the right we have all the contents of your consciousness at a given time. These include not just the objects and properties which feature in your visual experience, but *everything* your consciousness contains – thoughts, mental images, sounds, bodily sensations, smells, the lot. On the left is the awareness which is apprehending all these contents.

Now, if consciousness in general has this awareness-content structure, the question arises as to where the self or subject (or *you* or *I*) fit into the picture. One answer to this question is that the subject just *is* the awareness. After all, aren't experiences things we have, and isn't the 'having' of a sensation equivalent to 'being aware' of it? This conception of the self as an *awareness*, a centre of experiencing, purely and simply, is often called the *Pure Ego* theory. This way of thinking about the self differs from that which Descartes defended because it does not claim that Egos are composed of some kind of non-physical stuff. On this view the self is *awareness*, purely and simply.[18]

The claim that we are things whose nature it is simply to be *aware* corresponds with how we generally feel or talk about ourselves. After all, during our waking hours we are always aware of something or other, and hence saying things such as 'The phone must have been ringing for some time but I only just became aware of it,' or 'My headache was so bad that I couldn't help being aware of it all the time.' In a different vein, the Pure Ego theory neatly sidesteps philosopher David Hume's complaint against the self.

Hume was a notoriously hard-line sceptic, who insisted that unless a claim could be backed up with observational evidence it should not be taken seriously. He argued that no matter how hard we introspect, we only ever find various kinds of experiential contents – auditory, visual, tactile, etc. – and no matter how hard we try, we never find anything in our experience which could plausibly be construed as a self. Supporters of the Pure Ego theory point out that Hume was wrong to expect to find the self in this sort of way. The fact that you can't see your eyes doesn't mean that you don't have any. If the self is that which is *aware of* the contents of our consciousness – if it is the thing to which these contents are presented – it clearly isn't going to appear *amid* these contents.

Furthermore, since the only essential property possessed by a Pure Ego is awareness, there is no obstacle, in principle at least, to an Ego of this sort moving from one body to another, or indeed from one psychological system to another. Have we stumbled across a viable competitor to C-theory?

Self-unification

Unfortunately, the picture isn't all rosy for the Pure Ego view, for it has at least one very unappealing feature. Being immaterial, Descartes' selves are immune to gunfire and disease (unlike our material bodies), but there is something they cannot survive: dreamless sleep. Pure Egos are similarly vulnerable. If we lose consciousness we lose all awareness. Since Egos just *are* awareness, the loss of consciousness is fatal to them.

The Pure Ego entered the picture in the first place because it supplied us with an account of the unity of consciousness. If we could account for conscious unity in another way, without appealing to the Ego, the main reason for positing the Ego would vanish.

In fact, we don't need to look very far to find an alternative, completely Ego-free explanation of the unity of consciousness. Think again of what the unity in your experience is like, of the way in which your bodily sensations, your conscious thoughts, are all *experienced together*, along with what you are seeing and hearing or smelling. The characteristic and defining feature of these complex states is that their parts are all co-conscious, i.e. they are all experienced *as* unified. If our conscious states are intrinsically unified in this manner – and they are – it looks as though there is no need for an on-looking Ego to provide or explain their unity.

This way of thinking about the unity of consciousness has had numerous advocates, but probably the most influential was William James, the great psychologist-cum-philosopher and brother to novelist Henry. In 1890 James published *The Principles of Psychology*, an intoxicating blend of psychology, physiology and philosophy. In the *Principles*, James tries to synthesize all the known scientific facts about the brain, the mind and experience. Sheer ambition aside, what sets James's attempt apart is how attuned he is to the nuances of experience, and his ability to describe them in vivid prose. It is thanks to James's *Principles* that we now think of consciousness as stream-like, and think of a baby's first experiences of the world as a 'blooming buzzing confusion'. In the opening paragraph to Chapter 9, 'The Stream of Thought', James offers these observations:

> Most books start with sensations, as the simplest mental facts, and proceed synthetically, constructing each higher stage from those below it. But this is abandoning the empirical method of investigation. No one ever had a simple sensation by itself. Consciousness, from our natal day, is of a teeming multiplicity of objects and relations, and what we call simple sensations are the results of discriminative attention, pushed often to a very high degree.

This theme is taken up again in his later writings – such as the 1904 essay 'A World of Pure Experience', where James describes his own philosophical position on the nature and structure of experience as a *radical empiricism*. So far as the Ego is concerned, James was at one with Hume: he believed it to be *simply nothing*, a windy and ineffectual intellectual aberration. Whereas Hume despaired of finding an Ego-free solution to the problem of the unity of consciousness, James did not. Hume's problem was simply that he hadn't been a sufficiently *radical* empiricist; he had not paid sufficient attention to what we really find in our experience:

> To be radical, an empiricism must neither admit into its constructions any element that is not directly experienced, nor exclude from them any element that is directly experienced. For such a philosophy, the relations that connect experiences must themselves be experienced

relations, and any kind of relation experienced must be accounted as 'real' as anything else in the system.

Put another way, when James introspects he doesn't find the collection of 'loose and separate' experiences that Hume claimed to find. Far from it. We don't just experience a cup and saucer; we experience the cup *sitting on* the saucer. When you see a dropped cup shatter on the floor, your seeing and hearing the smash aren't separate experiences, they are experienced together. For James it's obvious that there are relationships between the different parts of our consciousness, and, since these unifying relations evidently exist together within our experience, there is no reason why an empiricist can't acknowledge their reality. What all the more specific ways of being related have in common is that the items in question are experienced together, as parts of a single, more encompassing state of consciousness. Or, to use the expression we have already employed, these experiences that are unified in this way are *co-conscious* – a term that James himself used.

A superfluous Ego

So why does the notion that we are highly localized centres of awareness make intuitive sense if no such centres exist or are needed?

Ordinarily, we perceive our surroundings from the vantage point of a particular, and fairly small, location, namely that of our bodies. Our conscious thinking seems to take place in our heads, and we seem to look out on to the world from behind our eyes. So to this extent the figure on p.95, which reduces us to a pure disembodied awareness, does not correspond to our ordinary experience.

But this isn't to say that we can't imagine ourselves existing as a disembodied form of awareness. Probably the easiest way to do this is by imagining oneself reduced to a completely *bodiless point of view*. If you engage in this sort of exercise, you will find yourself imagining that *you* (in the form of a thinking subject) are located at the centre of your sensory field. You will feel that *you* are situated where you seem to be perceiving the world from. But this does not mean that you really *are* located there, in the form of a Pure Ego or anything else – remember the tale of the missing brain.

When it comes to our sense of where we ourselves, as conscious, thinking-perceiving subjects, are located, the actual location of one's brain – or whatever it is that is sustaining or producing one's consciousness – is largely irrelevant. If your consciousness is in fact being produced by a brain-in-a-vat, but this envatted brain is connected to your sensory system so as to enable normal communication with your body and your sensory organs, the character of your overall experience will be entirely unaffected by your brain's absence from your skull. You will still seem to be thinking your thoughts *in* your head, and gazing out at the world through your eyes, even though in reality your de-brained head is entirely empty.

So while the claim that we are localized centres of awareness *can* seem intuitively correct, this is not because it provides an accurate understanding of the structure of our consciousness. It is because we have a powerful instinctive tendency to feel that we ourselves are localized at the very *centres* of our perceptual fields, rather than nowhere at all (or somewhere else entirely).

Streams of experience

So much for the unity of consciousness *at* a time; we still have to look at the second half of the story: the unity and continuity of consciousness *over* time, as found in our ordinary streams of consciousness. C-theory relies upon the claim that the flow of our experience from moment to moment constitutes a distinctive form of mental continuity. Is this claim correct?

A necessary first step is clarifying the way in which our experience *is* continuous over time. The use of the term 'stream' in connection with consciousness has been common since James's *Principles*, where he deploys the now-famous term 'stream of consciousness':

> Consciousness, then, does not appear to itself chopped up in bits. Such words as 'chain' and 'train' do not describe it fitly as it presents itself in the first instance. It is nothing jointed; it flows. A 'river' or 'stream' are the metaphors by which it is most naturally described. (1890: 239)

A characteristic feature of streams and rivers is their continuity: they are everywhere in motion, or so it seems when we look at them. James goes on to suggest in 'A World of Pure Experience' that our experience is also continuous, and in a distinctive way: 'What I do feel simply when a later moment of my experience succeeds an earlier one is that though they are two moments, the transition from the one to the other is continuous. Continuity here is a definite sort of experience.'

Thus, if James is right, our streams of consciousness aren't just successions of experiences that are free from gaps or intervals when no experience is occurring. Rather, they consist of *continuously experienced successions*. And our experience often does seem like this. When we watch a river flowing by, or hear a succession of musical notes – or the same ongoing note – we feel each brief phase of our experience giving way to the next, in a seamless fashion.

Acknowledging the continuous character of our experience is compatible with acknowledging that our streams of consciousness also contain discrete, sharply delineated contents: a pinprick, the rat-tat-tat of someone knocking on the door, the flash of a light from a camera. James recognized this, but held that they no more rupture the continuity of consciousness than 'a joint in the bamboo is a break in the wood' (1890: 240). By this he means that a sudden discrete noise (say) takes place against a large mass of *other* forms of experience – your bodily sensations, your visual experience, your mood and trains of thought. The felt continuity, the felt flow of this great mass of background experience – the vast bulk of which we are not usually paying attention to – is not normally disrupted by the occurrence of bangs, flashes, twinges and the like.

A temporal paradox

If our streams of consciousness are structured in this way, then C-theory looks to have solid foundations, since our experience possesses deep and distinctively *experiential* continuity.

However, there remains a hurdle. What I have been calling the 'flow' of experience is nothing mysterious, consisting as it does of experiences of change and persistence. When you see the road at night streaming by, or a cyclist hurtling around a velodrome, you are directly experiencing movement, and hence change. When you hear an enduring noise you are experiencing *persistence* – something continuing on through time without changing – and the same applies when you lie in a bath and enjoy the ongoing sensation of warmth on your skin.

So far so good, but now the problem arises. The following three claims all seem to be true:

(1) Change and persistence both take time. A thing changes when its properties vary over time. If a house that is painted white today was blue yesterday, it has changed colour; if it is still blue it hasn't changed in this respect.

(2) Our immediate experience occurs in the present. We can remember the past, we can anticipate the future, but our immediate experience is confined to *now*.

(3) The present, properly conceived, is the instant
    that separates the past from the future. Hence
    the present does not extend any distance
    through time; it is a durationless –
    instantaneous – interface between the past and
    the future.

If (1), (2) and (3) are correct, then all our direct (live) experience occurs in a present which is momentary. Since
change and persistence unfold over extended intervals
of time, we would not be able to directly experience
them if our direct experience takes in only momentary
events. But we do. So we have a paradox. It seems that
our experience can't possibly be as it seems – can't be as
it *is*.

. . . and a resolution

Confronted with this paradox there are those who have
accepted that our experience isn't as it seems, and that our
streams of consciousness are composed of successions of
momentary phases, the contents of which are entirely
static, and hence that we don't see things move – or hear
notes of music – in the way that we seem to.

But this isn't the only way of responding to the paradox, and I don't think it's the best one. Let us set aside (1)
and (3), and take a closer look at (2), the claim that 'our
immediate experience occurs in the present'. How can
this point of view be reconciled with the claim that our

experience is always dynamic, always flowing? How can *both* positions seem so right?

The way to resolve the paradox is to accept that our immediate experience is *not* instantaneous, but in fact extends a brief way through time – far enough to encompass the changes we are able to apprehend directly. This interval doesn't extend very far through time, since our direct awareness of change doesn't extend beyond a second or so, quite possibly less. Think of what it is like to see a traffic light changing from red to orange to green; you perceive each transition, but by the time it turns to green, you are no longer *seeing* it as red, though you can remember doing so. Nonetheless, a second is very different from an instant. A second is easily long enough for change to occur and be experienced; an instant is not.

So, from an experiential perspective, what is seemingly 'present' is in fact *non-momentary*. The fact that the experienced present – the *phenomenal present*, as we can call it – can embrace temporally extended phenomena was first explicitly recognized in the nineteenth century by German psychologists. In an influential discussion in the *Principles*, James calls it the 'specious present', describing it as 'the original paragon and prototype of all conceived times ... the short duration of which we are immediately and incessantly sensible' (1890: 631). In another passage James is more expansive, suggesting that the phenomenal present

is no knife-edge, but a saddle-back, with a certain breadth of its own ... It is only as parts of this duration-block that the relation of succession of one end to the other is perceived. We do not first feel one end and then feel the other after it, and from the perception of the succession infer an interval of time between, but we seem to feel the interval of time as a whole, with its two ends embedded in it. (1890: 609–10)

James' talk of a 'duration-block' is a useful way of conceiving and visualizing the phenomenal present, as in the diagram below.

The rectangle represents a single phenomenal present, a temporally extended 'block' of experience. Real-life phenomenal presents are brief phases of entire streams of consciousness, and so (typically) will have complex and varied contents. But in the case depicted here, the content is quite simple: it consists of the seeing of an arrow-in-motion moving a short distance through space. Obviously, the *whoosh* of a real-life arrow-in-motion can't be fully captured in a static image, but it's easily imagined, and it's important that it is: for the content of a phenomenal

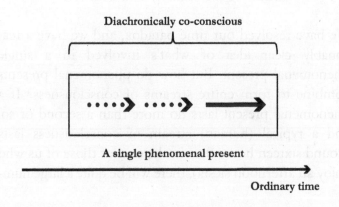

Diachronically co-conscious

A single phenomenal present

Ordinary time

present is usually *dynamic* in character. The bracket above the block is there to remind us that a single phenomenal present is a *unified* episode of experience. The whole thing is experienced *as* a whole, extending a brief way through time.

When discussing the unity of consciousness at a time, the sort which exists among simultaneous experiences, we used the term 'co-conscious' to refer to experiences that are experienced together in unified ensembles. Since the earlier and later parts of a phenomenal present are experienced together, are they also co-conscious? If we take 'co-conscious' simply to mean 'experienced together', then they are. However, they are not experienced together in the same way as in the at-a-time case. The experiential contents of phenomenal presents are experienced as *successive* rather than simultaneous. To mark this difference we can say they are *diachronically co-conscious*.

Building a stream of consciousness

We have resolved our time paradox, and we have a reasonably clear idea of what's involved in a single phenomenal present. But how do phenomenal presents combine to form entire streams of consciousness? If a phenomenal present lasts no more than a second or so, and a typical (human) stream of consciousness lasts around sixteen hours (less in the case of those of us who enjoy an afternoon siesta), there will be quite a large num-

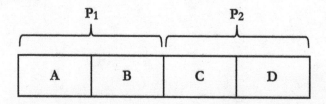

ber of phenomenal presents in a single stream. How are these episodes of experience related to one another?

One possibility is that successive phenomenal presents in the same stream exist side-by-side, in the manner of horizontal bricks. This sort of structure is depicted above. Here, A-B-C-D represent a succession of brief auditory tones that are experienced *as* a succession. A and B are diachronically co-conscious, and form parts of a phenomenal present P_1. C and D are also diachronically co-conscious, and form parts of the later phenomenal present P_2.

However, this combination of experiences doesn't in fact provide everything we need. If you were to hear the tone sequence A-B-C-D, you would hear A flowing into B, B flowing into C, and C flowing into D. The stream shown above includes the experience of A flowing into B in P_1, and C flowing into D in P_2. But there is no phenomenal present in which B is experienced as flowing into C, even though the transitions between *all* brief phases in a typical stream are experienced in the same way.

To accommodate the fact that B *is* experienced as flowing into C we need to introduce an additional phenomenal present, one which extends over both B and C, in the

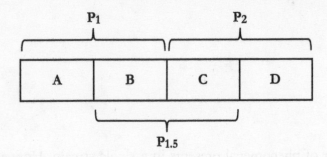

manner of $P_{1.5}$, above. In other words, we need to explicitly recognize that B and C are diachronically co-conscious.

It's important to note that when phenomenal presents overlap in this way it does not mean that everything gets experienced repeatedly. The experiencing of B which exists in P_1 and the experiencing of B in $P_{1.5}$ is *one and the same* episode of experience, with the result that B is experienced only once. Neighbouring phenomenal presents overlap by having parts in common. Similarly, if your garden and mine share a common wall, there is only a single wall dividing our gardens, not two.

Further, there is no need for phenomenal presents within the same stream of consciousness to be spaced out in *just* the way shown in the diagram above. Depending on how fine-grained our experience is – still an unresolved question – there could easily be a further phenomenal present extending from half-way through A to half-way through C, or from three-quarters the way through B to three-quarters the way through D. Irrespective of how closely packed these phenomenal presents are, since they overlap by part-sharing, everything is experienced just once, and not repeatedly.

We now have a coherent account of how our streams of consciousness can be as they seem to be. We can experience change and succession because these occur in phenomenal presents that are *not* strictly momentary, and our streams of consciousness can be experienced as continuous over long periods of time because they are composed of successions of phenomenal presents that overlap by sharing parts.[19]

Insights and implications

This way of conceiving the structure of streams of consciousness sheds new light on some earlier results. The U-SIM scenario outlined in Chapter 4 showed that when it comes to our continued existence over time our streams of consciousness are by far the most reliable guide. This insight was encapsulated by the C-thesis, which states that, for as long as our consciousness continues to flow, we continue to exist, irrespective of what changes befall us. The same insight was then used in the construction of C-theory. What distinguishes experiential capacities that belong to the same subject from those which don't is the ability to contribute experiences to the same stream of consciousness, or so I have argued.

This is placing a lot of weight on our streams of consciousness. Is the kind of unity they possess sufficient to carry such a load? Do we have a clear-enough understanding of streams of consciousness to be sure? In the absence of a credible account of the kind of unity and continuity streams of consciousness possess over time, such doubts would be quite reasonable. However, in the light of the account of stream-structure provided in this chapter, such doubts look to be misplaced.

Our main finding in this chapter is that streams of consciousness not only possess a genuine unity, this unity is a product of relationships among experiences themselves. Streams of consciousness may be produced by physical entities such as brains, or even immaterial entities such as souls, but their unity and continuity is a purely experiential affair. Moreover, there is no need to posit exotic entities such as Pure Egos to explain how the unity of consciousness comes about: our streams of consciousness (in effect) unify themselves.

7. What Matters (and Other Matters)

In this chapter we will be returning to where we began, by taking a closer look at whether teleportation is survivable. This question will shed new light on C-theory, and – more importantly – on what matters in life.

We will also broach the much discussed, but deeply puzzling, issue of what happens to a self that divides into two. As we shall see, these issues are all interrelated – but first things first.

Teleportation revisited

According to C-theory, you will be numerically identical with someone who exists at some future time only if there exists a potential for stream-like consciousness linking you to that person – or more precisely, if you are C-continuous with that person. Can the relationship of C-continuity be preserved by the informational teleportation procedure?

It seems unlikely. If you were to use this procedure in an attempt to cut down on the costs of transportation to Mars (say), to start with your body would be completely annihilated. You would then (in effect) be reduced to nothing more than a pattern of information encoded in radio waves, and it is these waves which make the trip to Mars – their journey can take nearly half an hour. When this radio signal is received on Mars, the information it contains is used to construct a replica of your body, as it was at the point of departure. Would you be C-continuous with this newly produced replica? Alas no. This is because a human brain has the capacity for producing experience but an encoded pattern of data in radio or light-waves does not – even if such data does permit the reconstruction of a physical brain that does.

So, by the lights of C-theory, this form of teleportation is not a way of getting around, it's a method of killing people.

This may be bad news for those of us who are weary of the drudgery of more conventional means of transport, but it could also be seen as bad news for C-theory. For there are those who argue that it would be crazy *not* to make full and frequent use of teleportation technology, if it were available, since it preserves everything that could possibly matter when it comes to our continued existence. This is the verdict Derek Parfit reaches in his discussion of teleportation in *Reasons and Persons*, when he is considering how to get himself to Mars:

> On my view, my relation to my Replica contains what fundamentally matters. This relation is about as good as ordinary survival ... ordinary survival, is, on my view, little better than – or about as bad as – being destroyed and Replicated. It would therefore be irrational to pay more for a conventional spaceship journey. (1984: 285)

Parfit is connected to his teleported Replica by causally underwritten psychological continuity, but not by C-continuity. If Parfit's relationship with his Replica is as good as ordinary survival then C-theory is in trouble. If C-theory is the correct account of our identity over time, then Parfit's relationship with his Replica shouldn't be anything like as good as ordinary survival.

And Star Trek?

So is Parfit wrong to claim what he does? I think so, and will be arguing as much over the course of this chapter. But let's begin by taking a closer look at a different – though familiar – mode of teleportation, that found in the various *Star Trek* TV series and movies. What does *Star Trek* teleportation involve? Would it be survivable?

Going solely by what one usually sees onscreen – a button is pressed, the transportee dissolves into a blur of lights, and then reappears *out* of a blur of lights elsewhere – it might well look as though we are dealing here with straightforward informational teleportation. If so, then C-continuity would not be preserved, and the procedure would be fatal. But in fact a lot more is going on than meets the eye.

The details are complex, but for our purposes it isn't necessary to venture into *Trek* lore concerning pattern buffers, Heisenberg compensators, phase transition coils, confinement beams and the like. The key point is this: in *Star Trek*-style teleportation, more is getting 'beamed' than a pattern of information. When an *Enterprise* crew-member seemingly dissolves on a transporter platform, their body is converted into a stream of particles – a 'subatomically debonded matter stream' to be precise – and, instead of being disposed of, these particles are themselves transmitted to the intended destination, where they are used to reconstruct an exact replica of the original crew-member as they were at the time of departure.[20]

This process differs significantly from informational teleportation, during which the original object is completely obliterated, and the resulting matter and energy are not sent anywhere. Since in *Star Trek*-style teleportation the re-created object is constituted of the same basic physical stuff as the original, a strong case could be made for thinking that this process successfully moves a single physical object from one location to another. After all, if your computer were dismantled into its component parts, and these same parts were later reassembled elsewhere, you would surely take the resulting machine to *be* your original computer. Isn't *Star Trek*-style teleportation just a more radical form of this way of getting around? It's a lot quicker, and the parts are smaller, but arguably the principle is precisely the same. If computers (or cars, or tables) can survive being dismantled into their constituent parts and then reassembled elsewhere, why can't we?

So far as our *personal* survival is concerned, the ability to transport physical objects is largely irrelevant. What matters is whether C-continuity will be preserved, and it is not obvious that it would be. Before the transporter device is activated you have a brain, possessing experiential capacities; a moment later you have been reduced to a beam of particles or energy speeding through space, and in this form you clearly don't possess any capacities for experience at all.

However, once again, all is not as it initially seems. There are a few *Star Trek* episodes in which we find out what it's like to be teleported from the first person perspective (e.g. *Star Trek: The Next Generation* 'The Realm of Fear'). Interestingly, it appears that the teleported subjects remain fully conscious *throughout* the process (e.g. seeing swirling coloured lights). A mode of teleportation which preserves the continuity of consciousness is obviously self-preserving.[21] Hence when Geordi La Forge says teleportation is the safest way to travel, in this context he's stating the truth, at least by the lights of C-theory.

What matters

The fact that C-theory is fully compatible with *Star Trek*-type teleportation being survivable undercuts one potential objection to it, but it doesn't help us in assessing the Parfit-inspired objection. Parfit claims that purely informational teleportation preserves everything that fundamentally matters in a subject's life. To be in a position to assess this claim we will first need to address a more basic question: what does matter in life?

Most of us have a special concern for our future lives and selves. This can be given a variety of labels, such as 'ego-centric concern', 'self-concern' and 'prudential concern'. (We also have a special concern for our past selves – e.g. I can only feel shame or pride in connection with actions that I have performed – but we'll be concentrating here on the future.) In fact, this self-directed concern comes in different forms and strengths, and is provoked by different sorts of circumstances.

If I know someone will be tortured tomorrow, I may be somewhat concerned; if I know that it will be *me* that will be tortured, I will be concerned in a very different – and very immediate – way. If I know that I will also be executed after being tortured, I will be very concerned indeed: I will experience the distinctive existential dread associated with the prospect of my own death or non-existence. There are also weaker, *merely preferential* concerns. I have spent a lot of time learning to play the piano well (say), and if some accident were to rob me of this ability I would be greatly distressed, but it wouldn't be the end of me – and I wouldn't fear losing this skill in the way that I would fear death or torture. Things which matter in the merely preferential sense are things we'd rather have than not, but the loss of which does not threaten our existence.

These familiar facts about self-oriented concern are easily explicable from the standpoint of C-theory. What I fundamentally am is a subject of experience; call this subject – the subject I am – S. If S exists in the future, then any experiences *it* has will evidently be experiences *I* have. Since I have a special concern for the quality of *my* experiences, I have a special concern for S, and I can anticipate experiencing what it experiences, and so will have a special ego-centric concern for those experiences.

From the vantage point afforded by C-theory, psychological continuity matters a great deal, but only in the merely preferential sense. Our memories, beliefs, values and personality traits are, on the whole, things we would prefer to keep, and would be distressed to lose, but we could survive without them. We will each of us survive only if the future contains a subject of experience with whom we are identical. Since any experiences these subjects undergo will be experiences *we* will undergo, our self-oriented concern naturally extends to them, and does so even if we are psychologically very different. Here the lessons of the thought experiments we considered in Chapter 4 are very relevant. As the U-SIM scenario illustrated, provided our streams of consciousness flow on without interruption, we continue to exist even if we undergo the most dramatic of psychological transformations – changes of a kind which rupture psychological continuity. If we can easily survive in the absence of psychological continuity, Parfit's claim that this is what fundamentally matters when it comes to our personal survival no longer seems plausible.

So far, so good, but an important issue remains. The idea that we will have a special concern for a future subject of experience with whom we are identical seems natural, but C-theory offers a particular account of what *makes* for subject-identity across intervals of time. You will be identical with some future subject if you are linked to them by an uninterrupted *potential* for experience, a potential which may sometimes be realized in actual experience, but which need not be. And that's not all.

C-theory tells us that selves are subjects, and that subjects *consist* of capacities for experience. Can *capacities* for consciousness engage our deepest concerns in the same way as actual streams of consciousness? Are such capacities things we can really care about?

There is every reason to think so. My consciousness is currently pain-free, but I can easily imagine it being otherwise. If I had a raging toothache, my experience would be a good deal worse than it is – and I'm mightily relieved that this sensation is *not* part of my current consciousness. To put it another way, I am relieved that the experiential capacity for this toothache is not active at the present time, for if it were, I would be suffering an intense pain in my jaw. The same applies to the other capacities which currently form part of my C-system: if they were active, the experiences they produce would (for better or for worse) be part of my current states of consciousness, and so my self-concern inevitably extends to them too.

The same applies over time. When it comes to experiences and experiential capacities that lie in the future, the points to bear in mind are these. Future experiences will have a subject. If I am that subject, then it's me that will be having the experiences in question. For me to care about those experiences in the special, self-interested way I care about my present experiences, or those I am about to have, then I must be able to make sense of the idea that the subject of those experiences really is *me*, rather than someone else.

C-theory provides us with a compelling account of precisely this. A future subject will be me if that subject is

C-continuous with me, i.e. linked to me by an uninter-rupted potential for consciousness. If this condition is met, I can be absolutely certain that this subject is me and no one else. I will have every reason to extend my ego-centric concern to the experiences this subject will have. I also have every reason to extend this same concern to the ex-periential capacities this subject possesses. For there can be no doubt whatsoever that it will be me who enjoys (or suf-fers) any experiences these capacities produce.

Psycho-copies

Bearing these points in mind, is Parfit correct when he claims that informational teleportation preserves what 'fundamentally matters', and for this reason is about as good as ordinary survival? In the light of what we have just learned, it looks very much as though Parfit is wrong. Informational teleportation certainly preserves psycho-logical continuity, but when it comes to our identity over time, this continuity isn't what matters. The relationship that *does* matter – the relationship to which our deepest self-oriented concern is inseparably tied – is C-continuity, which is *not* preserved by informational teleportation.

By way of a response, a defender of the psychological approach could try arguing along these lines:

> *Suppose in the middle of the night you are drugged and taken from your bed and put through a teleporter. The resulting replica – still sleeping – is put back in your bed. According to C-theory, the*

person who wakes up in your bed this morning isn't really you at all but an impostor. But isn't it clear that you are the person you think you are?

If events were to unfold like this, then the person who wakes in my bed would believe they are me – inevitably, since their psychology, memories included, is an exact copy of my own. But, as we all know, it is possible to be deluded about one's identity; the fact that this person believes they are me doesn't make it the case that they really are me. Recall our earlier example of the person who pops into existence as a consequence of an improbable quantum-mechanical fluke. By sheer chance, let's suppose this person happens to be an exact physical and mental duplicate of *you*. This person has apparent memories of your past, and believes they are you. Does the firmness of their conviction mean they are in fact you? Would you feel a self-oriented concern if you believed they were about to suffer a good deal of pain? I don't think you would.

The two cases are not entirely analogous. The psychology of the replica of me that was produced by teleportation – the *psycho-copy* as we can call it – is causally related to my own psychology, whereas the psychology of the freakishly produced replica is not causally related to my psychology at all. This difference is potentially important. According to Parfit, it is the relationship of *psychological continuity* which secures our identity over time, and psychological continuity is grounded in causal dependencies between earlier and later mental states. However, the form of causal dependency which exists in teleportation cases can easily seem quite insignificant – at least so far as our own survival is concerned.

To illustrate, let's suppose that I have acquired a Scan-&-Duplicate gun. This advanced piece of kit does what its name suggests. When I fire it at you, it performs a rapid and detailed scan of your body and brain; it then uses this information to create an exact psycho-copy of you just a few yards away. The scanning technology relies on a special kind of low-energy field which – rather like X-rays – do not harm you at all, and are entirely painless. It is entirely analogous to the replication process used in teleportation. When your psycho-copy pops into existence, and you turn to face them, would you feel prudentially concerned for their well-being and future? Would you feel *much* more concerned for the fate of this psycho-copy than the replica of you produced by a freak quantum occurrence? I strongly suspect not.

Protean selves

These various considerations, which all count against the survivability of teleportation, may seem compelling – they do to me, at least – but we aren't yet done. There is a further twist in the tale. A counter-argument can be formulated along these lines:

When in a piece of fiction we're presented with people who teleport frequently, and treat the process as survivable – as in Star Trek, *say – most of us can easily imagine ourselves adopting the same carefree stance towards the process. If we lived in a world where our friends and family were all regularly using teleportation to get around, wouldn't we find ourselves reacting in the same way? Isn't the fact that our intuitive response is so malleable, so easily influenced by narrative context, suggestive of the fact that there's no deep metaphysical problem with regarding teleportation as a survivable mode of transportation?*

That our views about the sorts of changes that are survivable for beings such as ourselves might themselves be susceptible to change, more so than we might suppose, has recently been suggested by philosopher Mark Johnston, in an intriguing discussion of teleportation in his *Surviving Death*.

Johnston argues that facts about our identities over time are determined to a significant extent by the ways in which we are disposed to identify our present selves with future selves. To put it crudely, if in your guts you *feel* that, yes, you *will* survive such and such a procedure, then you will indeed survive it – for it is these instinctive feelings that determine what you are capable of surviving. Johnston willingly concedes that we cannot change these identity-determining 'dispositions' (as he calls them) on a whim, but they are not immutable: with effort and training – a training which will likely involve a good deal of reflection on the metaphysics of the self and personal identity – it is possible for us to change the intuitive responses which help to determine the sorts of changes it is possible for us to survive.

As a consequence, or so Johnston argues, our essential natures are *Protean*:

> As with Proteus, who could assume the forms of a lion, a leopard, a serpent, or a pig, our essence could allow changes in our form of embodiment. The concrete embodiment of our identities as persons is in a certain way up to us to fill out; what we can survive, and the resultant facts of personal identity, are in a certain way response-dependent. (2010: 283–4)

If our identity-determining instincts and attitudes are Protean, by altering the relevant dispositions, such a person could come to feel that teleportation *is* something they could survive, and as a consequence of this change in attitude, this form of teleportation in fact *becomes* survivable.[22]

It may seem odd (to put it mildly) to suppose that the facts relating to what we can and cannot survive ultimately depend on what we think and feel. Can we really influence what we can survive (and not survive) in the way Johnston suggests?

Limits and metaphysics

Somewhere in a distant jungle there is, let's suppose, a tribal community who don't believe in souls of any kind, and who believe that death is normally followed by non-existence – with one exception: if a person dies by throwing themselves off a particular cliff on to the rocks hundreds of feet below, they won't cease to exist but will instead be reincarnated as a rock. As it happens, there is a particular variety of granite pebble which is highly regarded by the tribe. This belief is so deeply ingrained in their culture that those who are about to make the jump – as most do – are confident that they will survive. Happily, the granite pebbles in question are very numerous indeed.

To us, looking on from outside, the members of this community are obviously deluded: a person can't become a piece of rock. If souls existed, we might just be able to make sense of the idea that the soul of a person could move on to 'animate' a pebble, but that's not what is being envisaged here: the tribe don't believe in souls which can move from one physical body to another; they believe they will continue to exist as perfectly ordinary pieces of rock. Nor would the situation be changed if we all came to share the tribe's beliefs. Suppose a powerful but frivolous race of aliens, passing through our solar system tomorrow, brainwashes everyone on the entire planet, and we all end up believing we will survive our death by turning into pebbles. Would our deep conviction that such a transformation is possible mean that it actually is? Or would we simply be massively deluded?

When we think about this sort of case, that the facts about what we can (and cannot) survive are determined by what the majority of people believe seems plainly absurd. The aliens may have brainwashed people into thinking they can survive as pebbles, but this belief is delusory. There are, however, differences between this case and the kind

Johnston envisages. First, coming to believe we could survive as a rock requires a very large shift in attitudes; coming to believe we could survive teleportation wouldn't require such a dramatic shift. Also, Johnston doesn't envisage the change being brought about by brainwashing. The attitudinal change comes about as a consequence of our *reflecting philosophically* on what to believe about our survival conditions. And when it comes to the nature of the self there are very different views as to what the metaphysical facts are.

Johnston's views on this issue can be summarized thus: (i) we believe ourselves, fundamentally, to be centres or subjects of consciousness; (ii) we naturally believe these subjects persist through extended periods of time; but (iii) *this is delusion*, for there are no facts of the matter about the identities of subjects over time. Or as he put it:

> when it comes to our subjective mental identities over time – the supposed identities of THIS self, THIS consciousness ... we have not actually latched onto anything that would make for a determinate answer to the question of when we would have the same self, the same consciousness or the same arena of presence persisting over time.

Johnston allows that if we were immaterial souls of the kind Descartes envisaged, then there would be facts about our subjective mental identities over time, and these facts would tightly constrain our attitudes with regard to the kinds of changes (or methods of transportation) that we can survive. Since teleportation doesn't (presumably) transport immaterial souls, if we were entities of this sort then teleportation wouldn't be survivable. However, since there are no such entities – or so Johnston argues – there are no such facts.

Johnston may be right about there being no immaterial souls, but I think he is very much wrong about there being no facts about the identities of subjects over time. For, as we have seen over the last few chapters, if C-theory is correct in its essentials, then (i) we are indeed subjects of experience; (ii) there *are* facts about the identities of subjects of experience over time; (iii) these facts are determined entirely by experiential continuities – actual and potential; and (iv) these continuities are not preserved by informational teleportation.

What is more, as we have seen, the facts concerning experiential potentials (or capacities) which secure our identities are facts we very much care about, in a self-interested way. Since this is so, our attitudes regarding the sorts of thing we are, and the sorts of changes we can survive – teleportation included – will be just as profoundly rooted and difficult to modify as they would be if we were immaterial souls. The capacities for consciousness which are crucial to our continued existence can, after all, be kept in existence just as easily by a physical thing, such as a healthy living brain, as they can by an immaterial soul.

Bearing all this in mind, consider again the Scan-&-Duplicate device. If it is fired in your direction, and a psycho-copy of you is created, why does it seem so obvious that the copy isn't you? Why is it so difficult to believe the copy *is* you? I suspect that this is because the device succeeds in scanning your brain without in any way damaging it; you remain conscious throughout the procedure, you see the gun being pointed at you, and the replica being created shortly afterwards. It is because your consciousness *does* flow on without interruption that there is no room to doubt where *you* are. And it's because your consciousness does *not* move into the body (and psychology) of your replica that it is so very difficult to take seriously the idea that *you* do.

An asymmetry

We have little inclination to regard the psycho-copies created by Scan-&-Duplicate devices as anything more than copies. Yet what these devices do, at the mental level, is precisely what a teleportation system would do: conserve psychological connections. If the psycho-copies produced by Scan-&-Duplicate devices have no claim to be the original person, why should the psycho-copies produced by a teleportation system?

There is an important difference between the two procedures that we haven't yet considered. The Scan-&-Duplicate device leaves the original person intact, so we end up with two people who both have claims to be you. Since one of these people has your original body and brain, the situation is obviously asymmetrical: the claim of this person is obviously stronger. However, in the teleportation case, there's only ever *one* person present who has a claim to be you, since your (original) body is destroyed when the scan is complete. In the absence of any competitor with an unfair starting advantage, perhaps it is possible that teleportation *can* be survived.

The Scan-&-Duplicate scenario is indeed asymmetrical, but not in a way which ultimately assists the defender of the psychological account of the self. For, if psychological continuity was really sufficient to keep us in existence, then the Scan-&-Duplicate process would result in a genuine *splitting* of one's mind and mental life. To appreciate how far it falls short of this, let's look at another possibility.

The *Scan-&-Duplicate* II is a wonderful device which does what its predecessor could not: it causes the stream of consciousness of the person at whom it is directed to smoothly split into two branches, with one branch remaining in the original body, the other branch flowing into the newly created duplicate body. Now, in this case, if we stipulate that there is no disruption to the flow of experience in either branch, the outcome is very different: it seems clear that *you* both remain in your original body (with one branch of your stream of consciousness) *and* move into the newly created body (into the other branch flow).

This solves one problem – it's now clear how and why the standard Scan-&-Duplicate device fails to divide the mental continuity which matters – but it only gives rise to a further issue. If a person's life branches in this way, if a person *divides into two*, what happens to the original person, the one who divides?

Fission

Although C-theorists, Neo-Lockeans and animalists disagree about what makes for personal (or self) identity, they all agree that *some* form of continuity is normally sufficient for it: biological continuity for animalists, psychological continuity for neo-Lockeans, and an uninterrupted capacity for consciousness in the case of C-theorists.

As the Scan-&-Duplicate device shows, it is easy to imagine ways in which psychological continuity can easily branch. Teleportation accidents which result in two versions of the original person co-existing are a familiar plot-device in science fiction: the easiest way to achieve this is via a technical fault which results in the original person *not* being annihilated after their scan. So far as C-theory is concerned, what matters is whether streams of consciousness, whether actual or potential, can branch. It is certainly difficult for us to *imagine* a consciousness dividing. But what for us is unimaginable is certainly not always impossible.

Since the 1950s a good deal of research has been conducted on so-called 'split-brain' patients.[23] These are real people who have had their brains surgically divided – usually in an attempt to cure severe epilepsy – and lived to tell the tale. To be more accurate, the operation carried out involves the severing of the *corpus callosum*, the thick bundle of nerves which is the principal channel of communication between the two cerebral hemispheres. In the immediate aftermath of the operation many of the patients seem surprisingly unaffected by the procedure – or at least, going by their outward behaviour, it wasn't obvious that their brain had been divided. But further experimentation showed initial appearances to have been deceptive. Under controlled experimental conditions it is possible to communicate with each hemisphere separately; when this was done it quickly emerged that objects shown only to (say) the right hemisphere were not seen by the left hemisphere, and vice versa. The mental unity enjoyed by a normal subject had evidently been seriously disrupted, if not totally destroyed.

Precisely what kind of mental life split-brain patients have remains a subject of some controversy. However, it looks very much as though the *complete* division of a human brain into two functioning halves would yield two mental subjects – two C-systems – each enjoying an entirely distinct stream of consciousness. If these two half-brains were to be successfully transplanted into the (conveniently empty) heads of two otherwise normal human beings, the resulting people could function quite independently of one another.

So, surprising though it may seem, there is reason to suppose that our minds are capable of dividing into two, whether through a surgical operation, a faulty teleporter, or the Scan-&-Duplicate II.

Interpreting division

If fission is a possibility, at least from the vantage point of the mental continuity-based approaches to the self,

C-theory included, we need to be able to make sense of it. So as to bring the essentials into clear view we will focus on a single instance of fission, viewed in a schematic way.

Let's call the person who divides, A, and the resulting two people, B and C. To all outward appearances, we can suppose, each of A, B and C looks to be a perfectly normal person; the only thing which is at all special or distinctive about B and C is their history: they both originated from the splitting into two of a single earlier person, A. To simplify, we can further suppose that A is *fully* mentally continuous with both B and C, i.e. that A is both psychologically continuous and C-continuous with each of B and C. If we now ask 'What becomes of A when they divide?' there are four options:

(1) A is identical with B but not C.
(2) A is identical with C but not B.
(3) A is identical with B and with C.
(4) A is identical with neither B nor C.

The relationship which suffices for personal identity – call it R – holds fully and equally between A and B and also between A and C. Given this symmetry, it is unlikely that A is identical with just *one* of the people he or she divides into, but not the other; therefore neither (1) or (2) look very promising. We might be tempted by the third option, and hold that A is identical with *both* B and C. However, this would mean that just *one* person (A) is located at two different places, and has two different bodies and two different *minds* at the same time. It is not obvious, to put it mildly, that a single person can exist in such a fashion.

So we are left with the final option: we have to opt for (4), and conclude that A is identical with neither B nor C, and that the latter are two distinct people, just as they seem to be. But surely the relationship between A and B and C is too intimate for this to be the whole story? After all, A is continuous with B and C in ways which would ordinarily be sufficient for personal identity. Since A's mental life continues on in both B and C without interruption or degradation, the claim that A has simply ceased to exist does not ring (entirely) true.

In his influential discussion of this issue, Parfit argues that if we interpret fission cases in terms of identity then the fourth option is the best available: the original person ceases to exist when they divide, even though the original person is fully mentally continuous with both the people they divide into. So is fission fatal? Parfit points out that being confronted with fission is very different from being confronted with death: in the latter case your life ceases utterly; in the case of fission it not only continues on, it continues on twice over – a very different prospect! For Parfit, the fact that fission preserves mental continuity makes it (almost) as good as normal non-branching survival. It's almost as good despite the fact that identity is not preserved.

Parfit sees an important lesson here. Since personal identity and mental continuity normally accompany one another, it never occurs to us that our identity – and hence our continued existence – might have little or no significance. Reflecting on the case of fission teaches us that our own personal existence, our personal identity, is in fact of no intrinsic importance to us, contrary to what we naturally assume. What *does* have importance is the mental continuity which is fully preserved in fission cases.

Surviving fission: a gateway to metaphysics

The notion that our identity and what matters in life can come apart is certainly an intriguing one, but for Parfit's argument to be fully convincing we need to be sure that interpreting fission as equivalent to death is the only option. There are in fact several ways of construing fission as fully survivable. All that's required is some metaphysical boldness.

Think of how we ordinarily talk of species. If we saw a headline THE WOLF IS MAKING A COMEBACK IN RURAL FRANCE, we would have little difficulty in making sense of it: 'the wolf' in question is not a single individual wolf, but a higher-order entity – the wolf *species*. Mark Johnston has recently suggested that if we think of ourselves in this sort of way, as distinct species, or 'higher-order' individuals, we can think of fission as survivable. To illustrate, let's suppose Johnston himself divided into two yesterday, there are now two Johnstons walking the surface of the Earth: Johnston-1 and Johnston-2. Provided we think of Johnston as 'the Johnston' (species), he (or it) can be in many places at once in the manner of the wolf. So, although Johnston-1 and

Johnston-2 might give the appearance of being two distinct people, they are in fact different instances of *The* Johnston, one and the same species of person who existed prior to fission. So we have an alternative at our disposal: by thinking of persons as species, or higher-order individuals, fission becomes survivable.

Although thinking of ourselves as higher-order beings renders fission survivable in a simple and straightforward way, some might find the multiplication of distinct species it brings with it objectionable.[24] If you find yourself in this category, but you also feel that fission just can't be fatal, there is a further alternative – one that I have explored in detail elsewhere, e.g. Dainton (2008).

According to some interpretations of quantum mechanics, the entire universe is continually splitting (branching) into subtly different copies of itself. In effect, we are all undergoing frequent fissions, but since the resulting people end up in different branches of the universe they aren't aware of one another. Intriguingly, when contemplating *this* kind of fission, few people are inclined to regard it as fatal or life-threatening.

Now, a case of personal fission which involves just a single individual does not cause a branching of an entire universe. But it can be regarded as involving a branching in that individual's *personal time*. Personal time, roughly speaking, is the order in which events occur from the perspective of a given individual. Personal times do not usually diverge from the time of the world as a whole (i.e. objective time) but, under special circumstances, such divergences can occur. If we interpret fission in this way, the dividing person does not die; they continue to exist but their lives unfold in the different 'limbs' of their branching personal time.

A familiar example of personal time diverging from world time is created by time travel. When Doctor Who steps into the Tardis and travels into the past – to ancient Rome, say – does his arrival at his destination happen before or after his departure? The answer is both. From the perspective of his personal time, he arrives a short time after he departs; from the perspective of ordinary world time, the Doctor arrives many centuries before he departs. Time travellers who travel back and observe their earlier selves are also instances of a single person existing twice-over for the same period of *world* time. But here something unusual has happened to the personal time of the person in question: it has not branched; it has looped back on itself.

The tube of choice

Personal fission is a topic which has proven fascinating to those who are metaphysically inclined, and it has proved to be fruitful: pondering it has led to useful conceptual innovations.[25] However, it is not *just* an exotic metaphysical diversion. Fission-related considerations have led Parfit and others to conclude that personal identity and what matters in life can come apart, and hence that our identity – our continued existence – does not have the importance we naturally assume. As we have just seen, whether Parfit is right about this depends on how we interpret cases of fission, and this metaphysical issue is as yet unresolved.

In the earlier parts of this chapter we focused on the survivability of teleportation. We were led to this conclusion: opting to travel by this method would be risky in the extreme, at least for people like us. If the technology existed it would certainly be a very convenient way of transporting complex machinery, say, from one place to another. But one wouldn't send a valuable statue or painting through a teleporter – doing so would be a way of transforming your valuable original into an accurate but worthless fake. Nor would you send yourself.

From the start we have been focusing mainly on a single mode of teleportation: the informational variety, the process by which you are (in effect) reduced to a pattern of data that is beamed to a distant destination and then replicated. There were good reasons for concentrating on this mode of teleportation: the processes it involves are entirely transparent, and with the right technological developments it may actually be possible. However, this is not the only way in which teleportation, or near instantaneous transportation, can conceivably be accomplished.

A wave of a magic wand can instantly relocate a person elsewhere, by ensuring that the teleportation spell doesn't interfere with the teleportee's capacity for consciousness, and thus ensure their survival by the lights of C-theory. This may not be much of a consolation, magic being in short supply, but for the more technologically inclined, there is a staple of science-fiction literature which would offer the same happy outcome: travel by *wormhole*. A wormhole – in the physics literature they are known as 'Einstein-Rosen bridges' – is the name physicists give to a short-cut through the space-time continuum. We aren't yet able to manufacture wormholes, but physicists believe that the laws of nature governing space and time in our universe may well permit them.

The wormhole is a tunnel-like structure which connects two distant regions of our space, but does so without passing *through* our space at all. In seeing how this could possibly be, it helps to work with a space that has two dimensions rather than three, a space that consists (in effect) of a thin flat plane. A wormhole in this two-dimensional space is simply a tunnel which passes through the *third* spatial dimension (and so passes over or under the horizontal plane). Since we are unable to visualize a *four*-dimensional space, we can't mentally picture (or draw) wormholes connecting regions of our three-dimensional space in the same manner. But, mathematically speaking, such structures are possible. Moreover, it is also possible for the length of the wormhole to be far shorter than the distance separating its two ends in normal space. Again, this isn't something we can easily visualize, but it is physically possible – thanks to Einstein, we now know that space can be stretched and squeezed. Consequently, if locations that lie many miles apart in ordinary space could be connected by a wormhole of just a few feet, such a tunnel would provide a useful – and entirely safe – short-cut through ordinary space, making travel far quicker and easier than it would otherwise be. You wouldn't need to take a space ship to get to Mars (or the nearest star): you could walk.

In Chapter 1 we encountered one vision of an ideal future transport system. Just as today's internet traffic travels at light-speed through fibre-optic tubes criss-crossing the oceans, we dreamed of *people* being encoded as patterns of light, and carried through these same tubes. There are powerful reasons for thinking purely informational teleportation is less even than a dream. But if future technology makes networks of *wormholes* possible, the long-term future of tube-travel would be assured.

8. The Place of Mind in the World

If the conception of the self I have been defending and elaborating over the course of this book is along the right lines, then one thing is very clear: Descartes was right when he claimed that consciousness is the key to the self.

That said, if we adopt C-theory we are rejecting Descartes' claim that selves are always conscious. For us to continue to exist we needn't *actually* be conscious; it is sufficient for our capacities for consciousness to persist. However, it remains the case that we are essentially subjects of experience, beings whose *defining trait* is the ability to be conscious, just as Descartes claimed.

Descartes also held that minds in general, and conscious intelligence in particular, cannot be physical. Was he right about this too?

Many contemporary philosophers subscribe to 'physicalism', the doctrine that our universe is physical through and through. Since physicalists hold that mentality in all its forms is a wholly physical phenomenon, they claim that Descartes' additional world of immaterial minds is surplus to requirements. For the physicalist's conception of the universe to be viable, the arguments put forward by dualists – to the effect that the mental simply *cannot* be physical – will have to be countered, and we will be looking at the prospects for this shortly. The proponents of physicalism also argue they have a far better account of how minds and bodies can interact than dualists.

We'll make a start by investigating this last claim. As will soon emerge, although the physicalist does have advantages on this front, the situation is less cut-and-dried than is sometimes assumed.

Causes and ghosts

If you decide to turn on the radio in order to listen to some music, your decision – a mental occurrence – results in a series of physical occurrences: your hand moves in the direction of the radio and presses a button. Let's suppose that your listening to the music triggers feelings of pleasure and some happy memories. If so, then a sequence of physical events – the vibrations in the air produced by the radio, vibrations in your ear-drum and electro-chemical changes in your brain – has produced a series of *mental* events, in the form of your enjoyable experiences.

In everyday life our minds and our bodies are interacting in all manner of ways, all the time. Realizing this, Descartes advocated 'interactionist' dualism, which permits two-way causal transactions between immaterial minds and material bodies. But while this form of dualism is well-motivated, it also gives rise to a worry. Is it really possible for *non-physical* things to causally interact with physical things?

Consider ghosts, a commonplace example (at least in stories and movies) of a kind of thing whose nature is most definitely non-physical. If a ghost were to threaten to punch you in the face, you might be dismayed to have upset a denizen of the spirit-world, but the prospect of the ghost's fist hitting you would cause you no concern. After all, if the punch were thrown it would pass right through your body – just think of the way ghosts can pass through walls. Ghosts (probably) don't exist, but they do point to a problem for Descartes: if it is impossible for immaterial ghosts to bring about changes in the physical world, won't the same apply in the case of immaterial minds?

By way of reply, Descartes pointed out – quite correctly – that not all forms of causation work by brute physical contact. If by a wave of his wand a wizard changes an irritating child into a toad, there is no physical contact involved: the magic acts directly. Nor need we confine ourselves to imaginary cases, for science provides us with examples of similarly direct forms of causation. Newton's gravitational force, for example, operates on distant material bodies *directly*, without any intervening mechanism: according to Newton's theory, the sun and distant planets and stars are pulling this way and that on your body all the time, and they exert this pull without physical intermediaries – there are no pieces of string-like stuff stretching through space connecting you to the objects that are exerting forces on you. Magnetic attraction works in a similar fashion.

If causation between ordinary physical entities can work in a very direct way, the dualist can reasonably ask whether there is any reason why a similarly direct form of causation between *mental* and physical entities should be ruled out as utterly unintelligible or impossible.[26]

Interactions between immaterial minds and physical bodies can seem problematic for other reasons. Physicalists point out that if minds can produce changes in the physical world – and in fact are doing so all the time, as we move our bodies – then the physical world is not closed off from non-physical influences. They go on to argue that as things currently stand there is no scientific evidence of *any* non-physical influences on neural events in our brains; neuroscientists have yet to detect neurons in human brains behaving in ways which cannot be explained in terms of ordinary physical causes. But, again, this is far from being a knock-out blow. Dualists accept that *at present* there is no evidence of non-physical events on our neural systems. But currently our fine-grained knowledge of how our brains work is very limited. As our understanding of our neural processes improves, it may become apparent that there are in fact changes in our brains which cannot be explained in purely physical terms. Physicalists are very sceptical about this, but it may be decades (or even centuries) before we are in a position to know if their scepticism is justified.

Is the situation an evenly matched stand-off? Not quite. Physicalists have a further card up their sleeve – a powerful one.

Drones and drunkenness

Military drones have introduced a new dimension to the practice of war, and given rise to new issues in the ethics of warfare. When soldiers send 'Remotely Piloted Vehicles' into hostile territory, they can deploy the arsenal of deadly weapons their drones have at their disposal without fearing for their own personal safety. Equipped as they are with powerful radio communications technology and high-resolution cameras, drones allow their operators to take their time in finding their targets without worrying about whether they are about to be shot, blown up or fall victim to a poisonous gas attack. Since the operators are hundreds or thousands of miles away from the buildings or people their drones are targeting, any attacks on the drones themselves will not harm the people controlling them.

Interactionist dualism implies a similar relationship between immaterial minds and their bodies as exists between remotely piloted drones and their operators. Immaterial souls are not inside (or even near) their bodies, but they are nonetheless in communication with them. Through special causal channels connecting them to their brains, immaterial souls are able to discover what is going on in and around their bodies in real-time, and they are able to direct their bodies to move accordingly. Given this, our immaterial minds *should* also be as immune to physical assault as the remote drone operators. If a drone is shot at, say, and as a result slightly damaged, it will be more difficult to control. If some of its cameras are degraded, the operator will find it harder to 'see' what's going on in the drone's environment. But by virtue of being many miles away from the scene of the action, the drone's operator will be healthy and unharmed.

It is here that the analogy breaks down. Our minds are

very far from being invulnerable to physical assault. If you drink a sizeable quantity of alcohol, your brain's functioning will be impaired for several hours. The consequences are probably familiar. Your ability to control your bodily movements will be impaired (you might find yourself staggering about, say), and your senses are rendered less reliable than usual (e.g. you suffer blurred vision). These consequences do not strain our analogy: the remote drone operator faces similar challenges when trying to deal with a damaged craft. But the effects of alcohol do not end here. Your ability to *think* clearly is also severely impaired, and, more generally, your cognitive abilities are diminished. And that's not all. Alcohol also influences one's emotional balance, one's memory, and so on. These impairments go far beyond anything the drone-operator suffers.

Distilled forms of alcohol may be called 'spirits', but there is nothing non-physical about them: they are chemicals, and their effects on the brain are purely chemical. How then do they manage to wreak such dramatic changes in non-physical *minds*? How do everyday chemicals exert a profound influence on a non-physical dimension of reality?

It could be that minds are not related to brains in the way drone-operators are to their remotely piloted vehicles. Descartes, for example, concedes in his Sixth Meditation that 'I am not merely present in my body as a sailor is present in a ship' but rather 'I am very closely joined and, as it were, intermingled with it, so that I and the body form a unit.' But what does this 'intermingling' involve? Unfortunately, so far dualists have made little or no progress in finding an adequate answer to this question.

Even if such an account were available, the mental effects of the comparatively mild brain dysfunctions brought on by alcohol (and other recreational drugs) suggest that we need a properly functioning brain in order to think and reason properly. The cognitive consequences of brain disorders such as Alzheimer's disease are more dramatic by far, and all too familiar. It looks very much as though the immaterial soul is *incapable* of thinking and reasoning in the absence of a normally functioning brain. Not surprisingly, this fact strengthens the hand of those who claim that the soul is entirely redundant and that our cognitive powers reside entirely in our brains.

Neuroscientists would be the first to admit that far more remains to be discovered about the brain's functioning. At present we still have little idea as to precisely how the electro-chemical activity created by the billions of neurons in our heads gives rise to particular aspects of mentality. Nonetheless, thanks in large part to new brain-scanning technologies such as MRI, we now know, for example, which parts of the cerebral cortex are associated with our different senses, and which parts have control over our limbs. Within the visual cortex we know which sub-systems are responsible for perceiving shape, size, motion and colour. We know which part of the brain is responsible for facial recognition; surprisingly it has been found that very tiny clusters of neurons are triggered by specific faces (giving rise in some quarters to talk of a 'Jennifer Aniston neuron'). We know that damage to one quite localized region of the brain leads to the inability to understand language, whereas damage to a different region impairs language production. Our increasing understanding of the effects of neuro-transmitter chemicals, such as serotonin and oxytocin, has led to the development of mood-enhancing drugs, the potency of which is obvious to the millions who take them every day.

These discoveries do not completely settle the issue. The substance-dualist can respond by saying, 'Yes, the causal relationship between minds and brains *is* of a highly intricate sort, and so *of course* there are complex interdependencies between neural activity in our brains and those parts of the soul that are responsible for our sensory experience and higher cognitive powers.' But it is also fair to say that soul-theorists have yet to provide any details about this relationship, or explain how it takes the form that it does. In contrast, if we hold that our minds are not distinct from our brains, then it is not surprising that our mental functions are heavily dependent upon our brains. In themselves these interdependencies may not prove that the mind is the brain, but they are precisely what one would expect to exist if the mind *were* the brain.

Turing contra *Descartes*

We will have to wait for neuroscience to advance from comparative scientific infancy to adulthood before it becomes fully clear whether our brains really are capable of sustaining all aspects of our mental lives in the way physicalists claim, and this may take a while. In the meantime, scientific advances in a different field have already had a significant impact. These advances have gone a long way towards undermining one of Descartes' two main arguments for rejecting physicalism.

As we saw in Chapter 2, Descartes claimed the following:

(1) Like all living things, our bodies are nothing more than machines, composed of physical parts.

(2) No machine could possibly replicate our intellectual capabilities.

(3) So our higher mental capacities must reside in something *immaterial*, something which does not suffer from the limitations of physical machines.

If our bodies are machines, it is hard to comprehend how their internal mechanisms could produce the endlessly variable and creative behaviour of the sort we can deliver when we engage in everyday conversation, let alone when (on those rare occasions) one of us manages to produce a great work of literature, or a breakthrough in advanced mathematics. A sufficiently intricate mechanism might be capable of mimicking some of our abilities, over a narrow range of circumstances, but it is difficult to see how any clockwork sort of mechanism could possibly replicate the *boundless* character of our intelligence.

Or, at least, that was the case until computers entered the picture. Artificial intelligence has not developed at the same rate as computational hardware, which continues to double in power every two years, but it has nonetheless made very considerable advances. Google's computer-driven cars are now legal in California – though they still have to have a human passenger on board, just in case. The 'Deep Blue' chess computer made headlines by defeating the then-world champion Garry Kasparov in a six-match series; today's best chess programs are far more advanced than Deep Blue and routinely beat the world's best human players.

The ability to comprehend natural language has long been a serious hurdle for artificial intelligence, but there has been progress on this front too. The US game show *Jeopardy* has an unusual gimmick. Rather than contestants being asked questions to which they have to supply the answers, in *Jeopardy* contestants are provided with answers to which they have to supply the questions. A typical answer-cum-question might be: 'This drug has been shown to relieve the symptoms of Attention Deficit Disorder with relatively few side effects', and the correct *Jeopardy* response would be 'What is Ritalin?'. In a recent contest against the two most successful human *Jeopardy* contestants in history, IBM's 'Watson' computer came out on top. In so doing Watson demonstrated an impressive comprehension of language, and the ability to make fast and effective use of the vast pool of information IBM engineers put at its disposal.

In 1950 the mathematician, code-breaker and computer pioneer Alan Turing published a paper in the philosophy journal *Mind*, in which he addressed the question of whether or not a suitably programmed digital computer could ever really be intelligent. In this paper the famous Turing Test for artificial intelligence was introduced. The essence of the test is simple: all that a computer has to do to be considered intelligent is pass itself off *as a human person* when conversing (via keyboard and screen) with another human person. Since the human interlocutor is free to ask questions on anything and everything – from 'What did you have for breakfast yesterday?' to 'What do you think of the humour in Shakespeare's sonnets?' – the challenge is far from trivial.

It may well not be coincidental that Turing's test requires a truly intelligent machine to do precisely what Descartes claimed a mere machine could *never* do.[27] In his paper, Turing predicted that a digital computer would be able to pass the test within fifty years: 'at the end of the century . . . one will be able to speak of machines thinking without expecting to be contradicted'. He may have been optimistic in his predictions. We have entered the second decade of the twenty-first century, and a computer has yet to pass the Turing Test; Descartes was right – giving a machine the conversational powers of an average human *is* a difficult challenge, harder by far than beating world chess champions or winning at *Jeopardy*.

However, despite this failure, we need to bear in mind that artificial intelligence is still in its infancy, barely having celebrated its half-century. Also, as the success of Watson demonstrates, very real advances in language-handling have been made. If the current rate of progress continues, it may not be very long before a computer succeeds in doing what Descartes claimed to be impossible.

In the meantime, one thing is clear: it no longer seems *inconceivable* that a mere physical thing could possess cognitive capabilities which rival or even surpass our own.

Of course, digital computers are very different from human brains. Computers are powered by silicon chips containing vast numbers of transistors and other electrical components – just over a billion in the case of an Intel quad-core i7 processor. Human brains are composed of around three pounds of living grey tissue with the consistency of tofu. As uncomplicated as brains may look, a typical one contains 80–100 billion brain cells, or neurons, and each of these neurons is connected to hundreds or thousands of other neurons to which they transmit electrical (and chemical) signals. The total number of inter-neuronal connections in a typical brain is estimated to be 10^{14}–10^{15}, i.e. between a hundred and a thousand billion *billion*. It is not for nothing that our brains are frequently said to be the most complex objects in the known universe.

Their sheer complexity is one of the main reasons why there is so much we have yet to learn about how brains work. And we will have to know far more about how they function before we can be certain that our cognitive abilities do depend solely on neural processes. As of now we can say this much: the silicon chips which power our current computers are comparatively modest devices, at least when their physical complexity is compared with that of human brains. So, if these silicon chips can possess glimmerings of intelligence, there is every reason to suppose that our brains can possess somewhat higher levels of intelligence – little reason, indeed, to suppose human levels of intelligence are beyond them.

Consciousness: still the hard(est) problem

What of Descartes' second main argument for dualism? Have scientific advances also undermined the reasoning which led him to conclude that *consciousness* cannot be part of the material world?

As we saw earlier, Descartes' conviction that consciousness could not be physical is rooted in the austere conception of the basic nature of material things which he and the other scientific revolutionaries endorsed. One of the key advances of the Scientific Revolution was the adoption of the atomistic and mechanistic conception of the physical world. Animating Scholastic forms were excluded from the physical realm as part of this move, but so too were all the phenomenal properties, the properties we encounter in our ordinary experience. According to the new scientific worldview, physical things themselves possess only 'primary' properties, such as mass, motion, charge, shape, and so forth. Material things *don't* possess experiential properties such as colour, sound, warmth or pain.

As Descartes was perhaps the first to appreciate clearly, if the physical world is as the new science says, experiences and conscious subjects are banished from it. In which case, dualism – in some form – seems to be unavoidable.

The problem contemporary physicalists face is that Descartes' conception of the physical world is still very much with us. Thanks to advances in science the *range* of basic physical properties has expanded somewhat – to include electric charge and nuclear forces, for example – but if you were to leaf through a modern text on fundamental physics you would not find any mention of experiential properties. So the main barrier to the integration of consciousness with the physical world remains fully in place.

The bolts of lightning that rip through a stormy night sky are powerful and terrifying. Our ancestors believed them to be manifestations of divine fury. But we now know they were wrong: science has revealed that lightning is merely an electrical discharge, and we have a very successful scientific theory of the nature of electricity. Living things seem so very different from non-living things that many of our ancestors believed there were two fundamentally different kinds of matter, one possessing a special vital animating force, the other not. But we now know they were also wrong about this: there is just one kind of matter, the difference between living and non-living things derives entirely from the different chemical processes occurring in each. The history of science is a history of *progressive demystifications*. If at present we are unable to account for consciousness in a scientific way, physicalists argue that we should not be perturbed: we have every reason to think that it too will fall under the embrace of science as science advances. Thanks to the Copernican revolution we were obliged to accept that the Earth is nothing exceptional, but human beings surely are. Or so it seemed natural to think until Darwin demonstrated that humans are just another animal product of evolution. By continuing to claim that consciousness cannot be physical, dualists are trying desperately to hold on to the notion that there is something special about us, something which distinguishes us from the rest of physical reality. If the history of science teaches anything, it is that there is nothing special about us at all – or so physicalists often argue.

But anyone who lays this charge at the dualists' door is overlooking a crucial consideration. The dualists' (strongest) reasons for claiming that consciousness cannot be physical are not just based on wishful thinking. What makes it so hard to see how consciousness could be physical is the austere conception of matter that lies at the very heart of the Scientific Revolution. Rigorously separating the properties which matter really possesses from the properties we find in our experience was a crucial step without which science could not have advanced as it did. But it has also made it far more difficult to see how our quality-laden consciousness can be a part of physical reality. Since this conception of matter is itself a product of science, the claim that there is something special about conscious beings such as ourselves has excellent scientific credentials.

Emergence (and its limits)

Descartes may have been an important scientific pioneer, but since the 1630s science has also seen significant developments, most of which he could not have envisaged.

Developments in computer science have made it easier to see how intelligence could be a physical phenomenon. Have any of the subsequent developments in other areas of science made it any easier to see how consciousness can fit into the physical world?

Properties such as *liquidity* and *solidity* are all physical properties, but you won't find any mention of them in a list of basic properties in a physics text. This is because liquidity is not a *fundamental* physical property but an *emergent* one; it is a higher-level property which comes into existence when very large numbers of atoms combine in certain ways. And, as we know from our chemistry texts, what makes the difference between a liquid and a solid is the kind of bond that exists between atoms. There are bonds between the atoms in a liquid, but they do not prevent the liquid's constituent atoms sliding past one another, whereas the atoms in a solid are more tightly bound.

Similarly, might *experiential* properties such as colour-as-experienced, sounds, itches and pains in fact be higher-level physical properties that emerge when lots of elementary particles are assembled in brain-like systems?

Over the years many people have been tempted to take this 'emergentist' line, but when looked at more closely, problems – of a fundamental sort – soon start to appear.

If you take a large number of physical particles and configure them into (say) a table, you have managed to create a new complex object with new properties. By virtue of having the structure it has, a table can do things (e.g. support a set of dinner plates) that its constituent particles can't do by themselves. However, no matter how you arrange or rearrange a collection of basic physical particles, one thing you won't do is to create any *new fundamental intrinsic qualities* over and above those which were already to be found in the original particles. If the original particles lack the intrinsic qualities in question, you won't bring these into existence by rearranging the particles into a new configuration or structure. Since the problem of consciousness lies precisely in understanding how the qualities we find in our experience can be present in physical things which are entirely lacking in them, it looks like we're no closer to solving our problem.

To illustrate, is there any way in which a group of colourless particles can be turned into coloured ones simply by being rearranged? If you had a magic wand to hand, there would be no problem: you could use a magic spell to conjure colour into existence. But physics rules out appealing to magic spells. If you are confined to the operations and transformations which physics recognizes, all you can do is move the particles around and change how they are connected to one another. There is no way in which *these* operations will result in colourless particles becoming coloured. This example is very much relevant for it is precisely colour (along with the other experiential properties, such as warmth, pain and sound) that we are seeking to account for in physical terms.

Physics does recognize that, under certain conditions, a particle of one type can be transformed into one or more particles of a different type (this can happen spontaneously, or when particles collide at high speeds). But, since the particles produced by such transformations only possess the kind of properties other basic physical particles possess – mass, shape, spin, charge, etc. – they too are entirely devoid of experiential properties such as colour.

What if you were to configure a collection of elementary particles so that they make up a living human brain? Would this make a difference? None whatsoever, and for the same reason. Particles which entirely lack phenomenal properties cannot suddenly *gain* these qualities simply by being put into a different configuration. Or, at least, not without the intervention of magic.

So the relationship between the physical world and consciousness remains deeply puzzling; indeed, it has often been said that this is *the* biggest remaining mystery of them all (though those working at the frontiers of cos-

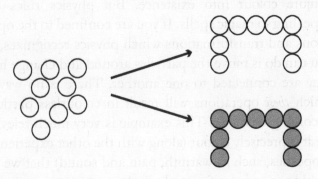

The quality problem confronting physicalism. It is easy to see how rearranging a collection of elementary physical particles can give rise to new *structures*, and the properties these structures possess (such as being able to support other objects). It is not easy to see how new intrinsic *qualities* such as colour can come into existence by rearranging particles which lack that quality in the first place.

mology and particle physics might want to disagree). But there is no reason to despair. As we will now see, there are at least two approaches to the problem of consciousness that are far from hopeless, and that do not suffer from the drawbacks of Descartes' dualism. While I do not think we are yet in a position to know which of these (very different) approaches is closest to the truth, I think both have very definite promise.

A naturalistic dualism

If phenomenal properties are distinct from and irreducible to any physical property, then some form of dualism is unavoidable. But Descartes' form of dualism is not the only form. In his influential *The Conscious Mind* (1996), philosopher David Chalmers explores a 'naturalistic dualism'.

Inspired by the remarkable advances in computer science, many have been tempted by the thought that our minds might be related to our brains in just the same way as computer software is related to the computer hardware it runs on. However, holding that our consciousness *is just* computational activity in our brains is problematic: it seems all too conceivable that this information processing could occur without giving rise to any form of consciousness at all. After all, there is no reason to think that when physical systems engage in information processing they acquire intrinsic qualities – of an experiential kind – in addition to the primary properties recognized by physics.

Although Chalmers rejects the simplistic computational account of consciousness just outlined (and for this reason), he also argues that the doctrine may not be completely misguided. Brains are the only physical systems which we are certain produce consciousness, and we also know that our brains engage in massive amounts of information processing, as our billions of neurons engage in their frenzied activities. Is this a coincidence?

Chalmers' positive proposal is that experiences are non-physical in nature and distinct from the computational activity in physical systems, but there is a law of nature *connecting* computational activity in physical systems and experience. This law is such that any physical system that has the same informational processing capabilities as a human brain will generate experience that is exactly similar to ours in character. So a sufficiently powerful and appropriately programmed silicon-based computer could be conscious in just the ways we are. Moreover, since there are many physical systems which engage in computational activity but are far less complex than human brains – e.g. rabbit brains, the computer chips in our phones – it may well be that these systems also produce experiences, albeit of a simpler kind.

Chalmers concedes that this theory is speculative, but it is certainly superior to other forms of dualism by offering a (comparatively) detailed account of the way in which physical activity can give rise to consciousness. Recently, neuroscientist Giulio Tononi has been leading an attempt to develop this sort of account in a more systematic way. Tononi (2008) argues that consciousness is related to the quantity of information in a system, but also, crucially, to the degree to which this information is *integrated* into a whole. He has developed a mathematical measure, Φ, for informational integration: the higher the Φ in a system, the higher its level of consciousness. Since introspection reveals that our consciousness *is* deeply unified – this is one of its most distinctive features – so too is the information it carries.

Cartesian dualism is embarrassed by the many and intricate ways in which our consciousness is dependent upon changes in our brains. Why do mood-altering chemicals affect our non-physical consciousness? Why does damage to one small area in the brain (the hippocampus) lead to an inability to lay down new memories? Why does damage to another (Broca's area) lead to severe linguistic impairment? Naturalistic dualists are embarrassed by these dependencies to a far lesser degree. For since they hold that consciousness is produced *by* computational activity in our brains, it is to be expected that changes in the brain which affect its computational activities will impact upon our consciousness in profound ways.

Descartes' dualism permits two-way causal interaction between minds and bodies. Bodily changes can produce mental changes (e.g. when we feel an itch in response to a skin irritant), and mental changes can produce bodily changes (e.g. when we decide to stop scratching the itch – and do so – because we remember that it just makes it worse). Chalmers' version of dualism allows physical events to bring experiences into existence – computational activity in the brain does precisely this. But it does not permit our consciousness to cause changes in the brain. Naturalistic dualists accept the doctrine that only physical events can be causes of physical events. By adopting this position the dualist avoids having to understand how non-physical things *can* causally influence the physical, so it has its benefits, but it also has counterintuitive consequences. Our conscious decisions never directly lead to actions, one thought can't lead to another in the sense of being the direct cause of another – the only things that cause thoughts are non-experiential events in our brains. When we move to scratch an itch, the cause of the bodily movement is not the itch *as felt* but some purely physical event in our brain.

On this view, our experiences – our entire conscious lives – are akin to a fireworks display: full of light, colour and sound, but ultimately *just a display.*

Conscious matter

There is another alternative on offer, one which does not deprive consciousness of the power to act.

It's hard to see how consciousness can itself be physical if physical things possess only the properties which physics says they do – properties such as mass, size, momentum, charge, and so forth. For as we have seen, it is very difficult to see how properties such as *these* can combine to constitute or create the phenomenal qualities we find in our everyday experience. There is a way around this difficulty: what we need to do is increase the range of properties that physical things can possess. We need to accept that at least some physical things have fundamental properties over and above those that can be found in particle physics textbooks. Moreover, given that we want to integrate the phenomenal and physical realms, these additional properties will have to be experiential in nature.

This approach is sometimes called 'Russellian Monism', since the influential philosopher Bertrand Russell advocated making this move in several of his works, including *The Analysis of Matter* (1927) and *Human Knowledge* (1948). In this passage Russell points out that the account of the physical provided by physics is very limited:

> Physics is mathematical not because we know so much about the physical world, but because we know so little: it is only its mathematical properties that we can discover. For the rest, our knowledge is negative … The physical world is only known as regards certain abstract features of its space-time structure – features which, because of their abstractness, do not suffice to show whether the physical world is, or is not, different in its intrinsic character from the world of mind. (1948: 240)

If Russell is right and physics (in its current guise) tells us about the *structure* of the physical world, but nothing at all about its intrinsic character, then for all we know – for all physics tells us – the intrinsic nature of some physical things may be experiential. This is precisely what Russell proposes.

Russell's claim that physics does not provide us with knowledge of the interior natures of physical things is far from idiosyncratic: it is widely accepted by philosophers of science that the properties recognized by ordinary physics are without exception *structural* and *behavioural*. All these properties do is capture and constrain the shape and size of particles, and how they are disposed to causally interact with one another. In the case of two hypothetical particles of types X and Y, a typical physical theory will tell us how large the particles are, what shape they have, and how massive they are (i.e. how much force it takes to move them at any given speed). It will also tell us how they interact with each other, for example that X-type particles attract Y-type particles with a force of magnitude F. But they don't tell us anything more. Physical theories are entirely silent about the intrinsic nature of X- and Y-particles, what they are like *in themselves*; or the character of the stuff that fills the regions of space that they occupy.

Now, it is reasonable to suppose that at least some of the basic ingredients of physical reality do have intrinsic natures. If they didn't, then physical objects – without exception – would be mobile clusters of causal potential, and nothing more. But a world in which everything is no more than a potential is a world where changes are confined to changes in potential, and where nothing *actually* happens at all.

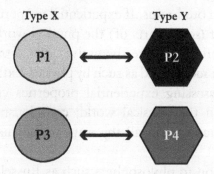

An illustration of how physics does not explain the intrinsic natures of particles, here represented by P1–P4. Provided P1 and P3 *behave* in the same ways when interacting with other particles, they will both be classed as being of physical type X, despite the differences in their intrinsic nature, here indicated by differences in interior shading. And similarly for P2 and P4.

We know that our experiences have intrinsic natures – colour and sound, etc., as they feature in our experience. So it may be that at least some of the intrinsic natures at the heart of the physical *are themselves* experiential. More concretely, there are certain physical processes in our brains – and those of other conscious beings – whose intrinsic natures are phenomenal. Or, to put it more simply, there are physical processes in us that are *conscious*.

The Scientific Revolution overturned our natural way of thinking by banishing sensory properties such as colour from the objects we perceive in our environments. According to Russell and his followers, the red we see a rose possessing does not exist on the surface of the rose, but (phenomenal) red does in fact exist within the physical world: it is an intrinsic property of certain neural processes in our brains. If experiential properties do lie at the heart of (some parts of) the physical world, then experiential properties are themselves *fully physical*, even if they are not recognized as such by physics textbooks. And entities possessing experiential properties can causally intervene in the physical world; consciousness can be causally efficacious in all the ways we normally assume it is.

In addition to philosophers such as Russell, Maxwell, Feigl, Lockwood and Strawson, there are also scientists who believe that to solve the problem of consciousness we will need to reject (in part) the austere conception of the physical world that was part and parcel of the Scientific Revolution. One such is Arthur Eddington, whose observation of a solar eclipse provided the first empirical confirmation of Einstein's General Theory of Relativity. In his wide-ranging *The Nature of the Physical World* (1928) Eddington argues that, counterintuitive as it may seem, physics has nothing to tell us about the intrinsic nature of physical things: what physics does do, with impressive accuracy, is develop a mathematical framework for coordinating and predicting measurable physical quantities. Since physics is entirely silent about the inner nature of material things, he can see no reason for supposing that these natures are incapable of constituting conscious subjects and their experiences:

> But what knowledge have we which renders it at all incongruous that they should constitute a thinking object? The Victorian physicist felt that he knew just

what he was talking about when he used terms such as *matter* and *atom*. Atoms were tiny billiard balls, a crisp statement that was supposed to tell you all about their nature in a way which could never be achieved for transcendental things like consciousness, beauty or humour. But now we realize that science has nothing to say about the intrinsic nature of the atom. The physical atom, like everything else in physics, is a schedule of pointer readings. The schedule is, we agree, attached to some unknown background. Why not then attach it to something of a spiritual nature of which a prominent characteristic is *thought*? It seems rather silly to prefer to attach it to something of a so-called 'concrete' nature inconsistent with thought, and then to wonder where the thought comes from . . . *There is nothing to prevent the assemblage of atoms constituting a brain from being of itself a thinking (conscious, experiencing) object in virtue of that nature which physics leaves undetermined and undeterminable.* If we must embed our schedule of indicator readings in some kind of background, at least let us accept the only hint that we have received as to the significance of the background – namely, that it has a nature capable of manifesting itself as mental activity. (1928: 259–60, italics in the original)

In talking of the 'background' here, Eddington is referring to external physical reality itself, *our* reality, which physics describes in purely abstract and structural terms. In suggesting that physical reality has a 'spiritual' nature he means, as he later makes clear, that it has a nature that 'is not altogether foreign to the feelings in our consciousness'. So, while elementary physical particles may not have the type of experiences that we do, their nature allows them to *combine* to constitute experiencing subjects such as ourselves.

And the self?

What are the implications of the differing ways of conceiving the relationship between the physical world and consciousness for the nature of the self, our *own* nature? According to C-theory we are, fundamentally, subjects of experience in the form of C-systems, which in turn are collections of experiential capacities with the distinctive attribute of being able to contribute to unified streams of consciousness. This account of the self is to a large extent neutral with regard to the issue of the precise relationship between the physical and the experiential. Irrespective of whether experience itself is physical or non-physical – an issue which remains contentious, as we have seen – that *capacities* for producing experience exist is not in dispute, and these capacities are all C-theory needs. That said, the differing views on the relationship between the physical and the experiential do influence the ways in which selves are related to the rest of reality.

If substance dualism is true, then the overall situation is very much as Descartes claimed. If experiences are non-physical, and capacities for experience reside in immaterial substances, along with our other mental capacities, then C-systems themselves are entirely non-physical. We have physical bodies, but what makes a particular body belong to me rather than you (say) is the existence of causal connections between my self and that particular body.

If Chalmers-style naturalistic dualism is true the picture is very different. Experiences are non-physical, and so do not exist in physical space. However, it is physical things – and not immaterial substances – which possess the *capacities* for consciousness. For in our universe there are basic laws of nature governing the generation of experience. The laws are such that experience comes into existence when computational activity is performed by physical systems, with different kinds of information-processing producing different kinds of experience. According to this version of dualism our streams of consciousness are non-physical, but the C-systems which produce them are firmly embedded in the physical world. Ultimately, we are hybrid beings, with one foot in the material world and one in the immaterial.

If Russellian monism is true the situation is different again. Experience is entirely physical in nature, and experiential capacities are possessed by physical systems. Both experiences and the experiential capacities which produce them are physical in nature. We are as fully a part of the material world as any other physical thing, even if we are distinctive by virtue of being conscious.

As we will see in the next chapter, these different views have very different implications for the future of selves. But, before exploring these new questions, a short detour is in order.

Zombie selves

Over the course of this book I have appealed to quite a wide range of creatures from fiction or fantasy: intelligent parrots, aliens, sentient computers, elves, ents and vampires. Some may be wondering: What's wrong with *zombies*? Why haven't they figured at all? At the time of writing, zombies are certainly much in vogue – in TV shows, movies and video games – and people who become zombies certainly undergo radical physical and mental transformations. However, they *are* more problematic, and in two different ways.

First, when it comes to precisely *what* zombies are, or how one becomes a zombie, there is a good deal of divergence. The traditional Haitian zombie is a corpse that is reanimated by voodoo magic, and which remains under the control of the sorcerer who brought it back to (quasi-)life. The zombies inspired by Romero's *Night of the Living Dead* (1968) are flesh-eating monsters motivated solely by their limitless hunger. Romero-zombies aren't created by voodoo: a bite from one of them is enough to transmit an infection which (vampire-like) brings about the transformation. These differences aside, quite what is going on in the mind of a zombie is unclear. The situation with vampires is very different. Vampires, as everyone knows, are non-human creatures, but their minds are essentially unaltered by their transformation.

The second and more important problem posed by zombies is that the term has a special use in philosophical

170

circles. So far as behaviour, inner physical constitution and outward appearances go, a *philosophical zombie* – and these are the only ones we'll be concerned with henceforth – is indistinguishable from a normal human being. But there is one difference, and an important one: they entirely lack consciousness. They are devoid of conscious thought and sensory experience of any kind, although you'd never guess this by observing them. Since they are behaviour-ally indistinguishable from a human, they talk about all the things a normal human talks about; since we often talk about our experiences, zombies do likewise – even though they don't actually have any.

Zombies have figured frequently in recent discussions about the matter–consciousness relationship, and it's not difficult to appreciate why. If it is possible for there to be a being which is indistinguishable in *all* physical respects from a normal human being – brain included – but which entirely lacks consciousness, then it's difficult to see how consciousness can itself be physical. If it *were* physical, then anyone who is an exact physical duplicate of you would also have the same sorts of experience as you. So if zombies *are* possible, consciousness cannot be physical, some of dualism would be true, and Descartes would stand vindicated.

Zombies pose a threat to other theories of mind too. Suppose advances in nanotechnology make it possible to replace the neurons in our brains with silicon-based replacements which exactly replicate, on the physical level, all the information-processing functions of the bio-logical originals. Suppose too that several of your friends have already made the switch to these longer-lasting and more reliable brains, and outwardly at least they are unchanged, and none have reported any untoward mental consequences – they all claim their experiences are just as vivid as they ever were. Would you follow suit and make the switch? Or would you have serious concerns? You might well, particularly since you know that zombies also talk about how vivid and wonderful their experiences are, despite the fact that they lack them entirely. If you believe that it's *possible* that your silicon-brained friends are zombies, then you should reject accounts of the mind which hold that mental processes are nothing more than computational processes. For, according to this view, a transformation that preserves the information-processing capacities of your neurons (which the envisaged nano-transform does) cannot possibly affect your mind in any respect.

When David Chalmers defended a version of dualism in *The Conscious Mind*, he did so, in large part, because he could see no good reason for supposing zombies are impossible. If zombies *could* exist, then it is difficult to see how any physicalist theory of the mind could be true.

The topic has featured less prominently in the recent literature, but zombies can also shed useful light on issues relating to the *self*. Suppose zombies are possible. For present purposes it doesn't matter if they have flesh-and-blood brains in the way we do, or brains made of some other kind of material; all that matters is that they are behaviourally indistinguishable from a typical human being, and that their behaviour issues from the complex information-processing systems in their brains – and not some 'deviant' source, such as a magic spell, say. We can now pose the key question: if zombies of this sort existed, would they be *selves*?

You might be tempted to think not, that they are merely mindless simulacra, things which are going through the motions of being selves, but aren't really selves. You would certainly be correct in thinking that they are not subjects of experience, since they don't have experiences, in any shape or form. But to dismiss them as *mindless* would, arguably, be wrong. Zombies lack consciousness, but in other respects they are very remarkable entities. The typical table also lacks consciousness, but its behavioural repertoire is rather limited; it's good for remaining in one place and eating dinner off, but not much else. In contrast, a zombie is capable of acting in all the ways in which a typical human being can act. In addition to being able to move around, zombies can also hold intelligent conversations, solve problems in creative and imaginative ways, tell jokes, learn new skills and languages, appreciate music and art, write novels, be loyal (or disloyal) friends, and much more. So far as their outward behaviour is concerned, they are capable of everything *we* are capable of (save for their complete lack of consciousness).

Rather than holding that zombies are mindless, it would be better to hold that they have a *distinctive kind of mind*. And these distinctively minded beings are also a distinctive kind of self. Since they do lack consciousness, no (conscious) self would regard a zombie self as being equivalent to a normal self. Zombies claim to have feelings and sensations – along with conscious thoughts and memories – but all they really have are non-conscious states in their information-processing systems that they *call* 'feelings', 'thoughts', 'memories', and so on. A zombie will say that it is in pain if it breaks a leg, but in reality it feels nothing; the same goes for zombie declarations of passion, or disgust, or outrage. Given all this, there are good reasons for regarding zombie selves – and lives – as possessing less intrinsic worth than normal conscious selves. But it is far less clear how much less worth.

The issue is further complicated by the fact that, if zombies of this sort *do* ever appear on the scene, then consciousness itself will suffer a down-rating in its importance. If non-conscious zombies can do everything we can do – if they are just as capable of creativity, imaginative problem-solving, affectionate friendships, acts of kindness, and so on – then it will look very much as though consciousness *per se* contributes little that is worthwhile or distinctive to a conscious subject's behavioural repertoire. If so, can it really be right to value it very highly?

One last point. We have seen that for conscious subjects such as ourselves travel by (informational) teleportation is a very risky proposition. It is otherwise with zombies. Since they lack consciousness, the successive phases of a zombie's life are not bound together by experiential continuity, whether actual or potential, so the fact that this form of continuity is ruptured by teleportation is of no significance for them. However, there is a form of mental continuity which does bind the successive stages of their lives: the causally grounded psychological continuity of the Neo-Lockeans. Provided we are prepared to grant that zombies possess psychological states at all, it is obviously possible for zombie memories and personality traits to be causally linked over time. And since psychological continuity *is* preserved in teleportation there is no reason why zombies need to seek out more expensive ways of getting around.

9. Future Selves

To conclude, I want to look at some further ways in which future technological developments may impact on our lives and selves. While we have already spent a good deal of time pondering exotic devices and transportation procedures, for the most part these technological (and magical) devices were introduced for an ulterior motive. There are various strands to a typical human life, numerous continuities and modes of connectedness. Some of these are relevant to our continued existence, others are not. The modes of travel we have been considering were introduced to allow us to isolate those continuities which are *most* relevant to our continued existence. Thinking about trips and transformations that we could or couldn't survive has helped us to discover the *kind of thing* that we are. As we have seen, we are essentially subjects of experience: beings whose sole essential property is the capacity to have experiences.

In this chapter we will be confining our attention to potentially transformative technologies which may well be *genuinely* possible in future, and so impact on real lives. These technologies have the potential to open the door to immortality (or something close to it), and to allow us to travel beyond the confines of this world. What is more, according to some of their more enthusiastic advocates, these technologies may well arrive far sooner than is usually supposed – in decades rather than centuries. While I am far from sure that these more optimistic forecasts are correct, I am by no means confident that they are not.

This alone is a reason for considering the technologies in question, but it is not the only reason. In assessing whether these dramatic transformations really are possible – possible *for us* – the nature of the self, and the issue of what sorts of change are survivable, are both very much relevant.

The transhuman

Orthodox medicine aims to cure diseases and bodily ailments, and minimize suffering. It has taken enormous strides forward in recent years, but there remains plenty of work to do. Is there room for a more ambitious approach to human well-being? Even if we manage to find cures for all the ailments we cannot now treat, human beings will continue to grow old, become frail and then die after only a few short decades. While this is the *natural* course for our lives to take, is it the inevitable one?

If the biological sciences continue to advance at their present rate, it may well not be long before it is possible – if we so choose – to dramatically increase our *healthspan*, the length of time for which we enjoy robust health. Given the choice, wouldn't most of us prefer to live two or three hundred years, or more, particularly if we knew that we would be disease-free, and have the body and mind of a twenty-five-year-old throughout? For this to be possible it will be necessary to modify our bodies in quite profound ways, at the genetic and bio-chemical level. However, thanks to anticipated developments in genetics, bio-chemistry, nano-chemistry and neuroscience, this is by no means out of the question.

For those in the transhumanist movement, this day can't come soon enough. According to their own FAQ, the movement 'affirms the possibility and desirability of fundamentally improving the human condition through applied reason, especially by developing and making widely available technologies to eliminate aging and to greatly enhance human intellectual, physical and psychological capacities'.[28] Transhumanists aren't content with merely improving our healthspan, for, as the philosopher Nick Bostrom puts it, they 'view human nature as a work-in-progress, a half-baked beginning that we can learn to remold in desirable ways'.[29] Hence their interest in human *enhancement*, in giving future humans – or 'post-humans' – superior physical and intellectual powers, not to mention an improved emotional makeup.

Francis Fukuyama has called transhumanism 'the world's most dangerous idea', and objects to it on ethical and political grounds. I am not going to enter into these waters here.[30] The question I will consider is straightforward: are the profound transformations the post-humanists have in mind changes of a kind that *we* could survive? To this question the answer is unambiguously 'yes'. If we are subjects of experience, our only essential property is our capacity for consciousness. Alterations to our DNA, or the nano-technological transformation – or even replacement – of our flesh and blood pose no threat to our existence, provided they do not interfere with this capacity.

In fact, C-theory is compatible with more radical transformations. We could survive enhancements to our intellectual and cognitive abilities, certainly, but we could also survive radical psychological transformations involving the wholesale manipulation or replacement of our beliefs, values and personality traits. In Chapter 4 we encountered the U-SIM, the gaming machine that allows the user to select the kind of psychology they want to enjoy during their virtual adventures; since subjects remain awake and fully conscious, their survival is assured. If it were developed, there is no reason why this technology need remain confined to the entertainment sphere: some people might opt to have their *actual* minds altered.

Massive psychological makeovers might not be to everyone's taste, particularly if the alterations are permanent. But if people's lives are much longer than our own, perhaps many times longer, some people might opt for it; what better way to stave off boredom?

From teleportation to speciation

If technologies which are capable of manipulating our minds in fine-grained and predictable ways are developed in the future, they are likely to affect the teleportation debate.

In Chapter 7 we encountered Mark Johnston's suggestion that our natures might be Protean, that by changing our philosophical beliefs and deep-seated instincts we might be able to change the kinds of transformations we could in fact survive, and thus the kind of thing that we are. The option of travelling by teleportation might open up for people who had previously regarded it as lethal. In response, I suggested that bringing about the required attitudinal changes might prove to be more difficult than Johnston himself envisages – and he acknowledges that it won't be easy. This may be how things stand at the present time, but it is easy to envisage someone arguing thus:

> *Yes, you may be correct when you say that our own self-oriented concern is locked on to C-continuity rather than psychological continuity, and that as a result teleportation would not preserve everything that matters to us. You might also be right when you say that bringing about a change in our attitudes and instincts, using the methods Johnston suggests, may well be beyond the capabilities of most of us: we can't voluntarily think ourselves into a state of mind – or being – in which psychological continuity alone preserves everything that matters. But future technological or medical developments are likely to make this irrelevant. In future it might well be possible to have one's attitudes with regard to what is survivable forcibly altered. A short course of advanced hypnotism might be all that's required – it may even be possible to get the job done by merely taking a pill.*

Since it is conceivable that attitude-changing techniques or technologies well beyond what are currently available will be developed in the future, it would be naïve to rule this possibility out. If such techniques *do* become available the prospect of stress-free travel by informational teleportation would become a reality for us all. Prior to taking the pill/being hypnotized the prospect of having one's body and consciousness obliterated is deeply terrifying, and the thought that one might survive as a mere psycho-copy utterly risible. But *after* popping the pill the landscape is transformed. The prospect of flicking the switch in the teleporter chamber now produces no trace of apprehension; and it seems just obvious that the resulting psycho-copy will be *you* and no one else.

Taking a step back, if these technologies were to be developed people would then have the option of choosing the kind of self they wanted to be. Human animals, subjects of experience and psychological selves of the Neo-Lockean variety are all rational conscious beings (at least in their normal adult guises), but they are nonetheless different types of self. What differentiates them are the sorts of continuity – biological, experiential and psychological, respectively – which is necessary and sufficient to keep them in existence. Because of these differences, each type of self has different persistence conditions: each has the capacity to survive different kinds of transformations. If the kind of self that *you* are is determined by your deepest beliefs and feelings regarding the kinds of change that *you* could survive, then by changing these beliefs and feelings it is possible to change the kind of self that you are, and therefore what kind of travel or transformation you are capable of.

There is no denying that altering profound aspects of

our psychological makeup gives rise to equally profound moral issues, and these will no doubt continue to be debated in the decades (and centuries) to come. Ethical issues aside, there may well be practical *dis*advantages to having these technologies at our disposal. To mention only the most obvious: the ability to survive one's bodily death by having a psycho-copy activated is itself likely to impact in all manner of ways on people's attitudes to (say) participating in dangerous sports, driving fast vehicles, or war.

So far in our history, 'speciation' – the process by which new animal species come into existence – has been a purely biological process, driven by natural selection. If the kinds of artificial biological enhancements the transhumanists are hoping for become possible, then biological evolution will no longer be driven by natural selection. But we can now see that there is another route to speciation, one that does not require profound *biological* transformations. All that is required is for technological developments to make it possible to alter our *psychologies* in deep ways.

If these developments occur, then even in the absence of biological enhancements in the future there may well be different types of human selves (or what started off as such) co-existing with one another. Some may take the pill and convert fully and completely to Neo-Lockean self-hood, and act accordingly. But others will decline the opportunity, and continue to take themselves – feel themselves – to be selves of a different kind: they will thus remain subjects of experience, or (just conceivably) human animals.

This mode of speciation will not be biological and it will not be driven by the random mutation of genes and natural selection. It will be driven – in large part – by purely philosophical reflection on the kind of self it is best to be. When it comes to evolution, philosophical deliberation and argument have their advantages over chance genetic mutation and natural selection, but whether its course is more predictable only time will tell.

Virtual heavens

Some futurologists – e.g. Ray Kurzweil and Hans Moravec – are eagerly anticipating something still more radical: the creation of computer-sustained virtual worlds into which people could 'upload' themselves and live out their lives.

Many of our present-day computer games already sustain quite large-scale virtual worlds, which players can wander around and explore. Although the virtual environments in the current generation of games are often impressive to look at, the role of the player is confined to moving a virtual character around with the help of a keyboard or control pad, or (more recently) by waving their arms about. What the proponents of uploading are looking forward to is being able to enter the computer-sustained world *themselves*, fully and completely. After completing the upload process, you won't be looking at the virtual world from the outside, you'll be right there *in* it, fully conscious, as a fully fledged participant, able to move your (virtual) body around at will. Like everyone else you meet on your virtual travels, your mind – your consciousness – will be being 'run' on the computer. You will, in effect, have left this world behind completely – or, at least, you won't be aware of it any longer. Your reality will be the virtual reality you have chosen to enter. But this world's lack of concrete physical reality won't matter: it will *seem* to be just as real and rich (or richer) as this world in every respect. The body you find yourself in will seem every bit as fleshy and physical as your current body.

If life as a virtual subject in a virtual world was limited to enjoying computer games, then the possibility of uploading oneself into these worlds would amount to no more than a more immersive form of escapist gaming. But the upload enthusiasts have something more ambitious in mind. They envisage entire civilizations existing in these virtual realms, comprising millions or billions of permanent inhabitants, people who live out their entire lives there. If computer-power continues to increase in the anticipated way – e.g. roughly doubling every two years, with more processing power packed into ever-smaller volumes – a computer capable of sustaining vast numbers of fully conscious virtual subjects, and the worlds they create, needn't take up much (real) space at all. Moreover, since virtual subjects are freed from the confines of the flesh, there is no need for nanotechnology to make a long and healthy life a possibility; they can survive in whatever form they choose as long as there is energy to power the computers which sustain them – many billions of years, at the very least.

These virtual civilizations will have the equivalents of public spaces where people can meet and converse, just as in our world. But, whereas the design of buildings in our world is constrained by the gravity and the strength and cost of available raw materials, there will be no such constraints in virtual reality: the sole constraint will be the imagination of the virtual architect. We can scarcely dream of the wonders they might create. But as a virtual citizen you wouldn't *have* to spend all your time in these public spaces, you could – if you so chose – devote yourself to designing your own virtual worlds – you could opt to spend a century or two exploring higher mathematics with the aid of an augmented intelligence. Or, you could decide to spend a decade or two partying intensely; you'd no doubt find plenty of people to join you.

In short, virtual worlds offer lives that are indefinitely long and always healthy, and the freedom to do or create what one likes. They're very much like heaven, but without an overseeing and sternly moral God. What's not to like?

These scenarios may all sound far-fetched – no more than digital dreams – but the transhumanists have another card in their hand, in the form of the 'singularity'. The artificial intelligences (or AIs) presently at our disposal aren't very powerful: maths and chess, yes, pretty strong; general common sense, no. But they are gradually getting better. Suppose we arrive at the point where the AIs that we have designed and constructed can design other AIs that are more powerful than themselves, and each new generation of AI rapidly creates still more powerful AIs. If this were to occur, since each generation of AI is not only more powerful but faster, before long we would have an 'intelligence explosion', the result of which would be *super-intelligent* machines, AIs whose cognitive abilities are as far beyond those of the average human as the average human's are above an insect's.[31] These AIs would be so advanced we cannot begin to predict the impact they would have, or what they might decide to do – the future then becomes unknowable, in a manner analogous to the interior of gravitational singularities, otherwise known as Black Holes.

The ability to design truly powerful computers might always be beyond us, but it might not be beyond the more able descendants of an AI we can construct. The ability to construct virtual heavens, and technology which allows uploading, may not be beyond these super-intelligent machines.

Zombies in paradise

This may all sound too good to be true – and perhaps it is – but it would be a mistake to dismiss these scenarios as no more than outlandish. There are serious thinkers who take the singularity argument very seriously indeed (the *Journal of Consciousness Studies* recently featured an article on the topic by David Chalmers (2010), and twenty-six letters by scientists and philosophers responding to his arguments[32]). If super-intelligences do arrive on the scene and are willing to cooperate with us – and I for one would be wary of ruling this out – then all our normal assumptions about the pace of technological development would go out the window. The possibility of uploading oneself into virtual heavens has also been discussed in detail by serious-minded folk, e.g. Sandberg and Bostrom (2008).[33]

But let's take things one step at a time, and consider this crucial question: would the inhabitants of these virtual worlds actually be conscious? They are certainly very sophisticated pieces of software. Their programs, after all, might well be derived from detailed scans of all the fine-grained neural structures in a human brain, and they would have the same immense complexity as a brain. But they still consist of patterns of information flowing around the circuits of a computer. Does this *guarantee* that they will be conscious?

When it comes to the relationship between consciousness and the physical world, as we have seen, there are a number of competing views that merit taking seriously. When it comes to the kind of mental life the inhabitants of computer-sustained virtual worlds might enjoy, these competing views have very different implications.

For Descartes and the Cartesian dualists, our conscious minds reside in non-physical substances. If conscious minds are not actually part of the physical realm at all, it would be a mistake to assume that activity in a wholly physical computer could, in and of itself, constitute a consciousness or a conscious subject. The Cartesian view is thus very hostile territory for the would-be uploader; computational processes in physical machines are just the wrong kind of place for consciousness to exist. Even if the complex software creations replicated the behaviour of ordinary human people – they acted and talked like any of us, etc. – they still wouldn't and couldn't be conscious subjects. They'd be zombies, of the philosophical variety. Given their sophistication, it may not be wrong to hold that virtual zombies have a *mental life* of a distinctive kind, but it is entirely experience-free; it is not a mental life we could envisage ourselves enjoying.

One alternative stance on the mind–body relationship is Russellian monism. This view is resolutely *non*-dualistic: according to its proponents, experiences and experiential properties are fully paid up members of the physical world. How is this possible, given the absence of any mention of experiential properties in the textbooks of fundamental physics? It is possible because there is simply *more to* the physical world than is recognized by current physics, or so the Russellians maintain.

If this way of thinking about the relationship of consciousness to the wider world is correct, the prospects for digital heavens are not altogether eliminated, but they are greatly reduced. Human brains and silicon chips are obviously very dissimilar, physically and chemically speaking. The only physical processes that we know to be capable of constituting consciousness are those which are found in mammalian brains such as our own. There is, consequently, absolutely no guarantee that the information processing in silicon chips – or their future non-biological successors – will be capable of sustaining conscious minds of the sort we possess. It may well turn out that, in our universe at least, consciousness and bio-chemical activity are inseparably linked, so that you can't have one without the other. If so, then even if it turns out to be possible to construct artificial physical systems that can sustain consciousness, it is likely that they will run at roughly the same speed as our brains, and be about the same size, and have similar energy requirements. The notion that we could 'run' billions of people, at super-fast speeds, would turn out to be a pipedream.

The situation looks very different, however, from the vantage point of Chalmers' naturalistic dualism. On this view, you will recall, consciousness is not itself a physical phenomenon; experiences are immaterial in nature. However, the occurrence of experiences is correlated in a law-like way with certain sorts of physical processes. Since the processes in question are computational – they involve the manipulation of data or information in or by physical systems – there is no reason whatsoever why a thing has to resemble a human brain in order to be able to produce experience. Any system which can manipulate information in the right sort of way – in the way your brain does, for example – will generate experiences.

Now, if this view is correct, then the transhumanists and would-be inhabitants of virtual worlds can rest easy. If the technology becomes available, then virtual worlds – *virtual paradises* – filled with fully conscious beings, not zombies, will become a reality.

To upload, or not?

Let's suppose for the moment that virtual worlds containing conscious subjects are possible.[34] Would it also be possible for *us* to move into them? Here is one fictional depiction of the process from Greg Egan's 1997 novel *Diaspora*, during the initial (highly destructive) phase of an upload:

> Waves of nanoware were sweeping through Orlando's body, shutting down nerves and sealing off blood vessels to minimize the shock of invasion, leaving a moist pink residue on the rubble as flesh was read and then cannibalized for energy. Within seconds, all the waves converged to form a grey mask over his face, which bored down to the skull and ate through it. The shrinking nanoware spat fluid and steam, reading and encoding crucial synaptic properties, compressing the brain into an ever-tighter description of itself, discarding redundancies as waste.
>
> Inoshiro stooped down and picked up the end product: a crystalline sphere, a molecular memory containing a snapshot of everything Orlando had been.

Is it really possible for Orlando to survive having his brain cannibalized for energy? Will the virtual-Orlando be *Orlando*, or merely a facsimile of him? For the transhumanists, the situation is straightforward. The scanning procedure may be bloody and destructive, but it has resulted in a complete and accurate record of Orlando's neural states and processes, and this record can be used to produce a conscious subject, in the virtual world, whose psychology is that of Orlando. So Orlando survives uploading, and so would you, if you were to go through the same procedure.

The envisaged procedure is, in effect, informational teleportation. The only difference is that the duplicate wakes up to find itself in a virtual world, rather than the real one. However, as we have seen, there is a very large question mark over whether this procedure would result in *your* waking up. Since destructive scanning ruptures C-continuity, it would not be survivable. The person who wakes up in the virtual world wouldn't be you; they would be nothing more than a pale psycho-copy of you.

Could an upload procedure which preserves C-continuity be developed? The answer will depend on knowing how to answer questions about the relationship between the experiential and the physical that we don't yet know how to answer with any confidence. If Chalmers' naturalistic dualism is true, and consciousness is connected by laws of nature to patterns of information flow, then it may well be possible to engineer bridges between the real and virtual realities which do not rupture C-continuity. But if Russellian monism turns out to be correct, and our consciousness is tightly bound up with our brains, such bridges may well not be possible – even assuming machine-generated virtual worlds themselves remain possible.[35]

The simulation threat

Suppose that it *is* possible for advanced computers to sustain fully conscious subjects. Suppose that in the future vast numbers of these subjects exist, living all kinds of lives, having all kinds of experiences. No sooner are these

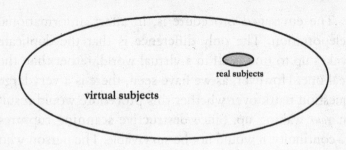

possibilities acknowledged than another possibility opens up. It could easily be the case that the total number of subjects who are computer-sustained virtual life-forms vastly exceeds the number of normal non-computer sustained subjects. Given this distribution – shown in the figure above – isn't it far more likely than not that *you* are already one of these machine-sustained subjects?

You may find this reasoning ridiculous. Won't these virtual subjects in the future be having amazing futuristic experiences, as they get on with living their enviably rich lives in their virtual heavens? Whereas we are living ordinary lives in the early years of the twenty-first century, having the (often dismal) sorts of experiences embodied human beings have during this period of history. So we know from the dated and dreary character of our experience that we're *not* among the many virtual subjects who will exist in the future. Or so you might be inclined to conclude.

However, this reaction overlooks two points. First, yes, many virtual subjects will be having experiences that are very different from those of a typical twenty-first-century person, but not all of them. It is possible that many will –

from time to time – indulge in finding out what life as a typically twenty-first-century person is really like, from the inside. Given this, it is possible that the number of artificially generated twenty-first-century-type streams of consciousness greatly outnumber the authentic articles. Second, a great many virtual streams (so to speak) will be purely fantastical or fictional, corresponding to no 'real' lives at all – after all, the inventive and creative powers of the machines of the future will be as incalculably immense as their purely computational capacities. Since (on current assumptions) the total number of virtual streams which will exist in the future is also immense, if the virtual environments these virtual subjects find themselves inhabiting are fictional, the odds are high that your current experiences fall into this category. If so, it's also likely that there is no twenty-first-century Earth at all.

It is important to appreciate just how powerful the most powerful computers of the future might be. Nick Bostrom provides a useful illustration: 'a rough approximation of the computational power of a single planetary-mass computer is 10^{42} operations per second ... Such a computer could simulate the entire mental history of humankind (call this an *ancestor-simulation*) in less than 10^{-7} seconds.' (2003: 247–8) Just to be clear: an 'ancestor-simulation' involves the simulation of the *entire* conscious life of *every* real human who has ever lived. Obviously, the simulators will have to rely on educated guesswork when it comes to simulating the lives of people who existed prior to the advent of accurate scanning technology, but this doesn't matter. If our descendants (whether human or machine) were able to run ancestor-simulations using only a small fraction of the computing resources available to them, they might very well do so, quite frequently. In such circumstances, the probability that you and I are inhabiting a computer simulation would be high.

Bostrom's 'simulation argument' takes the form of a trilemma. According to him we have to accept that at least one of the following claims is true:

(1) The human species is very likely to go extinct before reaching a technologically advanced stage.

(2) It is unlikely that any advanced civilization will run large numbers of simulations of their own history.

(3) We are almost certainly living in a computer simulation.

So if you are optimistic about the long-term prospects for humanity, and think that our descendants will develop and exploit simulation technology, then you will reject (1) and (2), and accept (3).

The many roads into the virtual

Perhaps you are confident that computational activity, of the sort digital computers engage in, cannot possibly give rise to consciousness. For better or worse, this does not mean that you can simply dismiss the simulation argument, for there are other ways in which virtual realities can be created and sustained.

Recall the U-SIM from Chapter 4. This advanced headset interacts directly with the brain, and has full control over the user's sensory experience, cognitive functioning and psychology. When attached to a suitable computer, it can plunge the user into virtual reality at the press of a button. It could provide you with inside knowledge of what it was like to be Napoleon at Waterloo, but it could just as easily provide someone living in 2300, say, with inside knowledge of what it is like to be an ordinary early twenty-first-century person, living through an ordinary twenty-first-century day. Even if computers *can't* ever be conscious, advances in neural-interface technology could provide another route into fully immersive, and fully life-like, virtual realities.

You might wonder why on Earth people living in the future would bother to spend their lives in the past. Surely they'd have better things to do? Again, this is a natural first thought, but I wouldn't place too much weight on it.

When virtual reality technology is far more advanced than it is today it will have so much to offer us that isn't available elsewhere. Consequently, it's quite likely that many people will routinely spend a fair proportion of their time in fully immersive virtual environments, just as today people spend a fair amount of time online. It's true, of course, that (most) people won't spend huge portions of their time 'visiting' the past, but they might well spend the odd hour or day there. These virtual reality trips to the past would certainly be used occasionally in history lessons, and future historians – amateur and professional – will no doubt make more use of the facility, as would novelists and others with a particular interest in what it was like to live at a certain period. But such trips might also be taken for entertainment purposes. The soap operas of the future might well have an immersive/interactive element that their present-day counterparts lack, computer games likewise. Already there is evidence that being able to enter and explore virtual worlds is likely to prove extremely popular. Over the past few years the number of people participating in MMPORGs ('massively multiplayer online role-playing games') has expanded dramatically – with the dominant *World of Warcraft* currently attracting around 10 million participants.[36] The addictive properties of these virtual worlds is well known; it is not uncommon for gamers to absent themselves from this world for hours per day. With the advent of fully immersive virtual reality technology, pastimes of this sort will probably prove to be more popular still.

With *lots* of people making even occasional virtual visits to the past, it's not difficult to see that the numbers soon add up. Most of us remain awake for around sixteen hours a day. Let's take streams of consciousness of this sort of length – we'll call them *D-streams* for short – as our working unit. Let's also say that a D-stream is *menacing* if it (a) exists in the future and is generated with the aid of a virtual reality system, and (b) is broadly similar in character to the streams of consciousness enjoyed by actual inhabitants of the early twenty-first century. Since a typical D-stream for a real early twenty-first-century person contains memories of that person's past life, menacing D-streams also include (apparent) memories of a past life. Menacing D-streams are carefully designed to conceal their real nature. Someone in the future who is embarking on one of these virtual trips to the past is provided with no clue that their experiences are anything other than what they seem to be, experiences that were actually had by someone living at the start of the twenty-first century. So it is quite conceivable that the experiences you will be having throughout today are, in fact, virtual.

Right now, there is quite a large number of genuine early twenty-first-century D-streams belonging to real people. If we assume the average population of the Earth from 2000 to 2020 to be seven billion, it turns out that there will be just over 2.5×10^{12} D-streams for any given year. In which case there will be around 50×10^{12} D-streams in total for this entire twenty-year period. For the simulation argument to bite, all that's required is for the number of menacing D-streams in the future to be roughly of this order. Just suppose that in the future the number of D-streams filled with experiences similar to those of an average early twenty-first-century person is roughly the same as the number of genuine, non-virtual early twenty-first-century day-long streams of consciousness. Since there's nothing special about your experience, there is a 50 per cent chance that *your* current experiences are virtual rather than real.

It is by no means far-fetched to suppose the requisite numbers of menacing D-streams, large though they are, might exist. The human population will very probably continue to increase, and increase enormously if we expand into space and colonize other planets, which in the centuries to come we may well do. Also bear in mind that we have centuries to play with. With a future population of (say) hundreds of billions, multiplied by hundreds – potentially thousands – of generations, all filled with people taking frequent virtual reality trips into the past, it is not implausible that the number of menacing D-streams will approach, and quite possibly exceed, the number of original D-streams. By way of an approximate comparison: think of how many people lived in the American Wild West in the nineteenth century, and how many people have lived there vicariously since then by watching them on TV or in movies. Moreover, as we shall see, there are reasons for thinking that visits to the early twenty-first century will be particularly popular among our descendants.

A novel predicament

A sizeable part of contemporary epistemology – the 'theory of knowledge' – is devoted to working out the best response to global scepticism of the sort Descartes wielded. What can we be truly said to *know* if we can't be sure that our thoughts and experiences are not all being produced by a malicious demon or mad scientist? At first view the epistemological consequences of the simulation argument may seem to be of just the same type: what we ordinarily take to be experiences of a real world may in fact be vivid hallucinations, in this case produced by machines in the far future, so can we really be sure of anything?

Descartes' demonic hypothesis is a *bare possibility* which we cannot rule out with absolute certainty, but have no particular reason to take seriously. The mad scientist feeding signals into our brains we are similarly unable to rule out, but also have no reason to take seriously. In sharp contrast, the hypothesis that you are living in a computer-generated virtual world is grounded in what may well be *reasonable empirical predictions* concerning the long-term prospects for humankind, and the likelihood of future technological developments.

Let's set aside bare sceptical hypotheses and suppose the world is much as you believe it to be, and what your ordinary experience suggests it to be; i.e. that there really is a planet Earth, and the course of human history is similar to what you've been taught at school. Let us also suppose that you believe, after deliberating long and hard on recent technological trends and human psychological tendencies, that it is probable that very powerful simulation technologies will be developed and used in the not too distant future. A dramatic consequence follows at once. If your careful reasoning leads you to these conclusions regarding technological trends, you should also believe that there is a significant probability that your own experiences are simulated. For if your beliefs about your world are true, simulated human lives will very likely outnumber non-simulated human lives.

This empirically grounded threat to our ordinary certainties is a very different beast to Descartes' demon. It's also a great deal more worrying.

Does the simulation argument undermine itself?

The fact that the simulation argument relies on predictions as to technological trends in the real world grants it an usual power and interest, but it also leaves it vulnerable to a potentially devastating objection. The simulation argument relies on certain supposedly accurate empirical predictions as to how the real world is likely to turn out. But if we come to accept that it is likely that we are living in simulations we obviously no longer have reason to accept the relevant predictions. There's no reason to suppose that future developments that seem probable from within a simulation are *really* probable. On this view, the simulation reasoning is self-defeating, and can therefore safely be dismissed.

At first glance this reasoning might seem to be compelling. The simulation argument is powered by the claim that there is a high likelihood that sophisticated technologies capable of producing and controlling experience will be produced and used in the future. If we come to believe that our own experience is being produced by one of these future simulators, then we no longer have any reason to believe that our own experience is a reliable guide to *anything*, let alone something as specific as future technological trends. In which case, the simulation reasoning does indeed undermine itself. So we can all breathe easily.

But not so fast. This objection itself relies on a crucial assumption, namely that the simulations that our descendants will use might be wholly *unreliable* guides to how things really are. Why think this? If our descendants are anything like us, a good many of the simulations they produce may well be complete fantasies which bear very little resemblance to reality. But equally, many – and quite easily the vast majority – will not be.

Simulations which are attempts on the part of future historians to faithfully recreate periods of the past (e.g. the twenty-first century) will obviously *not* be unreliable guides to the periods in question, far from it. But unless history proves more popular in the future than it has in the past, it seems safe to conclude that the majority of simulations won't be of the historical variety. Most of the simulations produced will very likely be more akin to works of fiction. Even so, a great many of the simulations that fall into this category will also be reliable guides to how things are. Not in all respects, but in all relevant respects.

When assessing the plausibility of the simulation argument, what matters are factors such as the following: in the real world, what are the laws of nature? What technologies do these laws make possible? What sort of people exist in the real world? And, if powerful simulation technologies are developed, is it likely that people will use them? Therefore, for a simulation to be *relevantly reliable* it will feature a virtual world that conforms to (apparent) natural laws similar to those that obtain in the real world, and it will paint an accurate picture of the broad sweep of social and technological trends during the relevant period – in our case, the early twenty-first century. Fidelity in matters of historical and biographical detail is not required. Nearly all contemporary novels – with the notable exception of most fantasy and some wilder science fiction stories – are relevantly reliable, despite the fact that most of the characters and events described in such fictions do not exist.

Taken together, these considerations draw much of the sting from the objection we have been considering. If you think it likely that many of the simulations our descendants will produce will be reliable in these relevant ways, then you can coherently believe that you are yourself living in one of these simulations. Also, and importantly, we have uncovered a constraint on the type of simulation to which the simulation reasoning applies. If you are led by the simulation argument to the conclusion that there is a fair probability that you are inhabiting a simulation, you have every reason to suppose that the non-simulated world is not *too* dissimilar to your world – in effect, you may be living in a fiction, but you are not living in a total fantasy.

An end of innocence

If our descendants do acquire the technological know-how to produce simulations, can we hope that they will choose not to make use of it? If the popularity of present-day role-playing games, rudimentary as they are, is anything to go by, our descendants are unlikely to deprive themselves of the more sophisticated diversions that simulation devices will bring. We should also bear in mind that simulation technology may well be in the hands of super-intelligent computers and so beyond our ability to control.

The news that it is quite possible that our lives are simulated will no doubt be received differently by different people. Some may welcome the idea that the life they are leading is only virtual, and that they will emerge from it (in just a few hours) to find themselves living in another century. For others, the news will be less welcome. There is also the issue that different types of simulation pose very different challenges. We might, for example, be living in a large-scale communal simulation of a large chunk of human history running on a massive computer. (In effect, this is the sort of simulation found in the *Matrix* movies.) If so, then you might reasonably react: 'So what? My friends and family are all real people; our experiences are as real as anyone else's. Our world may be virtual but it doesn't seem to be.' However, it could also be that your current experiences are being produced by a headset worn by a twenty-second-century teenager enjoying a history lesson, and the lesson is almost over. None of the people you take to be your friends and family are real; none will exist in a few minutes when the simulation ends.

There is a more general point of a philosophical nature to be made. Thus far in our history we have been able to rest easy in the knowledge that reality is, very probably, much as it seems to be. But the situation has now changed, and our age of innocence is drawing to a close. We now have to accommodate ourselves to the thought that, even if reality is much as it seems, there is still a significant likelihood that our current experience is simulated.

This disturbing thought may be news to many of us, but it is very likely not news to those born in more technologically advanced societies – and, if humankind has a long future, most humans will fall into this category. Having to live with the knowledge that 'all this is probably a simulation' may well be part of the normal lot of technologically advanced conscious subjects, whether human or non-human, biological or non-biological, the universe over.

This leads to another thought. Many of our descendants may want to escape the shadow of simulation and experience for themselves what it was like to exist in more innocent times, when it was possible to believe – really believe, down in the depths of one's heart – that things are as they seem. Living as they do in darker times, when this belief – this *state of being* – is no longer available, they will have only one option: to embark on fully immersive virtual reality trips into the past. This is bad news for our predecessors. The vast majority of people who *seem* to be living in innocent times may well be leading simulated lives.

Our own predicament is not much better. Many of our descendants might be tempted by the prospect of finding out what it was like to become aware of the simulation menace; experiencing the first falling of the shadow might prove to be an irresistible prospect. If so, life in the early twenty-first century may be an even more fragile thing than it appears.

Epilogue: On Being Moved
(or Not) by Time

Selves are things that exist in time. We are born, we die, and our lives are constituted by what we do and experience in the time between these two termini. While this much is obvious, what it *means* to exist in time also depends, in part, on the nature of time itself. This is a big and controversial metaphysical issue in its own right, and this isn't the place to explore the complex debates to which it has given rise, interesting though they are. But to appreciate how these debates impact upon the *self's* nature, it will suffice to have an overview of the main conceptions of time currently in play.

The most important of these are depicted in the figure overleaf, where each of the three solid shapes represents a very different way of thinking about the temporal character of the entire universe.

The thin solitary slice at the bottom of the figure represents the contents of our entire three-dimensional universe at the present time. The slice is two-dimensional (or close to it), so one spatial dimension has been suppressed. The longer solid in the middle represents our present, plus the entirety of the *past* – imagine thin cross-sections across this whole block (like the thin slice below it), each representing a momentary state of the entire universe at some past time. The still longer solid at

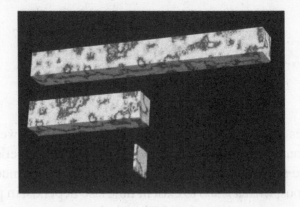

the top of the figure represents the *entire* universe, past, present and future.

Each of these views of the universe corresponds to a different conception of time itself:

(1) *Presentism (the small sliver)*: the universe consists of a succession of momentary (or very brief) phases; since only one of these presents is ever real, the past and future have no reality at all – they don't exist.

(2) *The Growing Block (the medium-sized solid)*: the present and the past both exist, only the future is wholly unreal; since new 'slices' of reality – new presents – are being created, and once created these remain in existence, the universe is constantly growing.

(3) *The Block Universe (the large solid)*: the past, present and future are all equally real; there is no privileged or moving present – every event

is present at the time when it occurs, just as
every *place* is a 'here'.

How does time differ from space? After a bit of thought, two important differences will probably come to mind: time only has one dimension, whereas space has three, and time passes, whereas space doesn't. That time *passes* seems obvious. We live our lives in the present, but the present is always *on the move*, or so it seems. If you find yourself looking at the clock and it says '10.35', we all know it won't be long before it shows a later time, and as for next Christmas, it's continually getting closer, minute by minute, second by second. The advocates of the Growing Block and Presentist conceptions of time both accept that time passes, but explain it in different ways. Conversely, proponents of the Block Universe deny that time passes. They believe that the character of our experience is such that it *seems* to us that the present is constantly changing, constantly advancing. But, they insist, this temporal passage is confined to these appearances; there is nothing in reality to which it corresponds.

If Presentism is true then our existence is confined to a brief, transient reality-slice in just the way it seems to be. As each present gives way to another, everything contained in those presents – our experiences included – are completely and utterly annihilated. As the present moves forward, in effect, we *ourselves* are carried with it. We are all, always, being transported into the future by the passage of time.

If the Growing Block account of time is the correct

one, our lives extend into the past, and the past parts of our lives – our past experiences included – are just as real as anything that exists in the present. But the future is entirely open: the parts of our lives that have yet to occur do not exist, in any shape or form – though this will change with the passage of time, second by second.

But if we inhabit a Block Universe, all the parts of our lives are fully and equally real. Although from the vantage point of the present we do not know what shape our lives will take in the future, or what sort of experiences we can look forward to living through, the future parts of our life – and the experiences and actions they will contain – are just as real as the present and past parts. On this view, we are four-dimensional beings, possessing lives which extend through time in much the way our bodies extend through space. Since we cannot visualize four dimensions, our true shape is literally unimaginable, strange though that seems.

Each of these competing views of time has their contemporary supporters, and the debates range over both metaphysical and scientific issues. On the metaphysical side, proponents of the Block Universe view often argue that the whole notion of temporal passage turns out to be incoherent when scrutinized more closely – a claim disputed by Presentists and Growing Blockers. Since Presentism and the Growing Block view posit a universe-wide privileged present to act as the interface between what is real and what is not, they require a wholly objective and universe-wide plane of simultaneity, and this does not sit well with Einstein's Special Theory of Relativity. According to this widely accepted theory, simultaneity is relative. People who are moving with respect to one another will find different sets of events to be simultaneous, and so disagree about which events are present and which are future and past. What is more, there is no fact of the matter as to which of these events *really is* present – all the various temporal perspectives are equally valid. Consequently, there is no fact of the matter as to where the dividing line between past, present and future really lies. In the light of this, many physicists and cosmologists lean strongly towards the Block Universe view of time.[37]

This notion that one's entire life is embedded in a timeless (or eternal) Block Universe can be an unnerving one. We may not know what the future holds for us, but since the future is just as real and fixed as the past, what lies ahead is already set in stone. But the Block conception also has its consolations. Shortly after the death of his lifelong friend Michele Besso in 1955, Einstein wrote the following to his family: 'And now he has preceded me briefly in bidding farewell to this strange world. This signifies nothing. For us believing physicists, the distinction between past, present and future is only an illusion, even if a stubborn one.' With this Einstein reveals a belief in the Block Universe; for him there is no difference between past, present and future. Anyone who is worried that death is the same thing as non-existence should welcome the Block Universe, for here lives have beginnings and endings, but they – with all their joys and sorrows intact – are forever part of an eternal four-dimensional cosmos.

In contrast, if Presentism is true, since the past has no reality whatsoever, then a second after your death you really will be gone: utterly, completely, and for good. Of course, depending on how you look at it, this view, too, can have its consolations.

Notes

1 The Dennett article in question is (not surprisingly) called 'Where Am I?', and can be found in his *Brainstorms* (1981), pp. 310–23. For additional discussion of the case, see 'The Missing Brain Case: A Closer Look' at the supporting website at www.barrydainton.com/self/. The site contains a number of excursuses relevant to the issues and themes we will be encountering over the course of the book – as well as some explanatory remarks on some relevant philosophical terminology.

2 In fact, this is the third of three 'laws' proposed by Clarke in his 1962 essay 'Hazards of Prophecy: The Failure of Imagination' (Clarke 1972). The first law is: 'When a distinguished but elderly scientist states that something is possible, he is almost certainly right. When he states that something is impossible, he is very probably wrong.' His second law is: 'The only way of discovering the limits of the possible is to venture a little way past them into the impossible.'

3 This view was 'new' in the sense that it was different from the received Scholastic conception, but it was not unprecedented in Western thought: the ancient Greek atomists subscribed to a similar theory.

4 Progress was of course swifter in some fields than others. Newton's *Principia*, published in 1687, provided us with laws of motion and a theory of gravitation that is adequate for (nearly) all practical purposes. It was only in the nineteenth century, with James Maxwell's discoveries, that we had an adequate theory of electromagnetism. And it was only with

twentieth-century developments in molecular biology that Descartes' contention that living organisms are merely (chemical) machines was finally vindicated – more on this shortly.

5 It may well have been Descartes' own view that when a soul becomes separated from its physical body it is henceforth confined to a purely intellectual mental life. There are also plenty of Plato-inspired Christian theologians who have taken a similar view. Not surprisingly, this abstract conception of the hereafter has not penetrated far into the broader consciousness. (Gustav Doré's illustrations of Dante's *Divine Comedy* better correspond with most people's conception of heaven.) It's also true, of course, that the purely intellectual view of the soul and the afterlife sits very uneasily with the thought experiments Descartes himself introduces, in which our mental lives – our streams of consciousness – continue on exactly as they are, with all their sensory aspects intact, in total absence of a physical world, brains included. In any event, the things that came to be known as Cartesian souls are immaterial minds that are capable of enjoying all the sorts of experience that we enjoy, both sensory and non-sensory.

6 Brevity is usually a virtue in philosophical writings, but often makes for interpretive difficulties, especially when the writings date from a few hundred years ago, and this certainly applies to Locke's writings on the self. A saying of Kant's applies here, as Strawson notes, 'It can be said of Locke's chapter on personal identity as "it can be said of many a book, *that it would be much shorter if it were not so short*".' (Strawson 2011: xiii)

7 What rate and depth of psychological change is compatible with survival? If we hold that psychological continuity makes for personal identity, what strength of psychological *connectedness* do we need from day to day, or month to month? Parfit suggests that

'there is enough connectedness if the number of direct connections, over any day, is *at least half* the number that hold, over every day, in the lives of nearly every actual person' (1984: 206). It could be argued that this is an arbitrary amount and that there will be borderline cases – for example, if you changed half of your beliefs, underwent a partial sexual reorientation, and lost quite a few memories but not all of them, then it's not clear whether your self survives or not. But Parfit's proposal provides a reasonable basis for a theory of our identities over time; and most accounts will give rise to difficult-to-resolve borderline cases.

8   For more on EPOC see www.Emotiv.com. At the time of writing, what the gaming community is *most* looking forward to is the release of 'Oculus Rift', the first audio-visual virtual reality system aimed at consumers – and hence at an affordable price – which promises accurate location-tracking (of one's head) and 3-D virtual environments.

9   Just how early in life do we begin to have experiences? Human foetuses are thought to acquire the capacity for rudimentary forms of consciousness between the 24th and 28th week of gestation. However, since normal foetuses spend their time in the womb deeply asleep, their capacity for consciousness is not usually activated prior to their birth – unless of course they *dream*, but whether they do is not yet known. For more on this see Koch (2009).

10   This section draws on Dainton and Bayne (2005).

11   That most people *do* in fact respond in this way to cases such as these is one of the several interesting and relevant points to emerge in a recent article by Nichols and Bruno (2010). That said, the explanation I am providing here of why our intuitions can be influenced by changes in narrative context differs from that supplied by these authors.

12 The magnetic potential in a Maglev track *also* persists through time, and does so continuously, assuming the track itself persists and remains in working order (the continuity would be ruptured by, say, a power cut). But since this cross-temporal continuity is less easy to visualize than its spatial counterpart it is less useful for illustrative purposes.

13 The theory is elaborated in most depth and detail in my *The Phenomenal Self* (2008).

14 There is a further difference. For Descartes, selves are akin to elementary physical particles, albeit immaterial ones; it is impossible for them to gain or lose parts in the way that compound objects do. There is no such constraint on C-systems. If someone loses their capacity for visual experience as a result of serious brain damage, they have lost an experiential capacity they previously possessed, and their C-system is diminished as a result; if thanks to some deft neurosurgery, a person who previously lacked the capacity for auditory experience gains it for the first time, then their C-system has been augmented. C-systems are in this sense *dynamic* or *mutable* in a way that Cartesian soul-substances are not.

15 It is also important to bear in mind that our mental cores – our C-systems – are not just composed of capacities for basic sensory experience. These do exist, but a typical human adult's capacities for consciousness are integral parts of a sophisticated psychological system. If this were not the case, our streams of consciousness would not be as rich, complex and varied as they are, containing (as they do) conscious thoughts – often in linguistic garb – along with memory images, conscious intentions, desires, strivings, fears and so forth. In the absence of a powerful cognitive system we would not be able to conceptualize our perceptual experience in the way that we do: a

new-born infant (or a dog) can visually register a tree they are facing, but they are incapable of seeing it *as* a tree. But all this complexity does not affect the basic picture. Cognitively sophisticated collections of experiential capacities are still C-systems, and the ability to contribute to continuous streams of consciousness is all that matters when it comes to assigning C-systems to persisting selves. I go into the relationship between C-systems and the rest of the mind in more detail in Chapter 6 of *The Phenomenal Self*.

16 'Our identity is the sum of our memories, but it turns out that memories are fluid, modified by context and sometimes simply confabulated. This means we cannot trust them and our sense of self is compromised. Note how this leaves us with a glaring paradox – without a sense of self, memories have no meaning, and yet the self is a product of our memories.' (Hood 2012: 59)

17 The use of the term 'content' in this context – i.e. as referring to parts or aspects of conscious states – can be puzzling when first encountered. But if a house or room can have contents, so too can our consciousness. The contents of your current consciousness consist of *everything* you are currently experiencing.

18 Though just to confuse matters, Descartes' immaterial self is often referred to as 'the Cartesian Ego'.

19 As with most (important) issues in philosophy, there are alternative views on offer. For a detailed discussion of the alternative conceptions of stream-structure, and a defence of the overlap account offered here, see Dainton (2006) and (2010a).

20 The relevant passage from *Star Trek: The Next Generation Technical Manual* in full: '**Energize and dematerialize.** The molecular imaging scanners derive a realtime quantum-resolution pattern image of the transport subject while the primary energizing

coils and the phase transition coils convert the subject into a subatomically debonded matter stream.' (Sternbach and Okuda 1991: 103)

21 Other good sources on *Star Trek* teleportation include www.calormen.com/Star_Trek/FAQs/transport-faq.htm and www.en.memory-alpha.org/wiki/Transporter.

22 In a similar, but more radical vein, anyone who believes that it is appropriate to identify with *all* future individuals (or at least, those who are deserving of such concern), and who also succeed in adjusting their identity-determining dispositions accordingly, will be justified in believing that they themselves will survive *as* these future individuals, in a quite literal way. Something approximating immortality is thus a genuine possibility for those who are suitably disposed. Johnston accepts that this route to immortality involves a considerable shift in how we think about ourselves, and won't be achievable by everyone – perhaps not by very many at all. But the shift required to believe that one could survive teleportation is comparatively small, and may well not be beyond most of us. In which case, if we do manage to make the switch, teleportation would actually *be* survivable, even though previously it wasn't. Johnston is not alone in defending this general approach to personal identity: see Miller (2004, 2012).

23 See Gazzaniga (2005) for further details regarding these experiments on split-brain patients.

24 Johnston's interpretation of fission is redolent of Scholastic metaphysics. The renowned medieval theologian Thomas Aquinas argued in his *Summa Theologica* that, since angels lack matter, in order to be distinct individuals – in the way your cat and table can be distinct – they must each possess a different essence, just as dogs (but not cats) possess *doggishness*, and hence

belong to a distinct *species*. There are thus as many distinct species of angel as there are individual angels.

25 Another way of interpreting fission as survivable is by construing dividing people as partially overlapping four-dimensional beings – see Sider (2002).

26 Scientifically informed readers will object at this point that, yes, Newton's theory of gravity does require action-at-a-distance forces, but Newton's theory was displaced by Einstein's General Theory of Relativity, in which there is no trace of Newton's action-at-a-distance force: gravitational effects are due to mass-induced distortions in the space–time continuum. And this is perfectly true. But the fact that action-at-a-distance forces *do* feature in Newton's theory illustrates that our conception of *physical* causation is broader than critics of dualism often assume. It should also be borne in mind that action-at-a-distance interactions may well be ineliminable from quantum theory. For more on this see http://plato.stanford.edu/entries/qm-action-distance/.

27 In this passage (from Part V) of his *Discourse on Method* Descartes sets out his case against machine intelligence: 'we can certainly conceive of a machine so constructed that it utters words, and even utters words which correspond to bodily actions causing a change in its organs (e.g. if you touch it in one spot it asks you what you want of it, if you touch it in another it cries out that you are hurting it, and so on). But it is not conceivable that such a machine should produce different arrangements of words so as to give an appropriately meaningful answer to whatever is said in its presence, as the dullest of men can do.'

28 http://humanityplus.org/philosophy/transhumanist-faq/.

29 See Bostrom's 'Transhumanist Values' at http://www.nickbostrom.com/ethics/values.html.

30 For more on this theme see Savulescu and Bostrom (2008).

31 Here's how mathematician and computer scientist Jack Good puts it in a 1965 article: 'Let an ultraintelligent machine be defined as a machine that can far surpass all the intellectual activities of any man however clever. Since the design of machines is one of these intellectual activities, an ultraintelligent machine could design even better machines; there would then unquestionably be an "intelligence explosion," and the intelligence of man would be left far behind. Thus the first ultraintelligent machine is the last invention that man need ever make.' The term 'singularity' was used by Vinge in 'The Coming Technological Singularity' (1993).

32 The responses to Chalmers (2010) are to be found in *The Journal of Consciousness Studies* 19 (2012), 1–2.

33 http://philosophy.ox.ac.uk/__data/assets/pdf_file/0019/3853/brain-emulation-roadmap-report.pdf.

34 The material in the remainder of this chapter draws on Dainton (2012).

35 Even if uploading *does* prove incompatible with preserving C-continuity, it may in the end not matter. From the standpoint of our present condition – of how we are presently constituted – it may seem clear that a rupture in C-continuity would terminate our existence, and that survival in the form of a psycho-copy would be very different from survival *per se*. However, if our natures are Protean, and technological developments make it possible to reconfigure our survival- and self-related feelings and attitudes, then a course of the right treatment could transform us *into* Neo-Lockean subjects. We could then confront the uploading process with equanimity, and digital paradises would be within our grasp. Provided of course that we were prepared to allow ourselves to be reconfigured in this sort of way.

36 According to a Blizzard press release, see http://us.blizzard. com/enus/company/press/pressreleases.html?101007. Over the past decade the number of subscribers at any one time has varied between 8 and 12 million.

37 I explore these different conceptions of time and the case for and against them in detail in my *Time and Space* (2010b).

References

Baggini, J. (2011) *The Ego Trick* (London: Granta).

Blum, A. (2012) *Tubes: Behind the Scenes at the Internet* (London: Viking).

Bostrom, N. (2003) 'Are You Living in a Computer Simulation?' *Philosophical Quarterly* 57 (211), pp. 243–55.

Chalmers, D. (1996) *The Conscious Mind* (Oxford: Oxford University Press).

Chalmers, D. (2010) 'The Singularity: A Philosophical Analysis', *Journal of Consciousness Studies* 17, pp. 7–65.

Clarke, Arthur C. (1972) 'Hazards of Prophecy', in *The Futurists*, ed. A. Tofler (New York: Random House), pp. 133–50.

Dainton, B. (2006) *Stream of Consciousness* (London: Routledge).

Dainton, B. (2008) *The Phenomenal Self* (Oxford: Oxford University Press).

Dainton, B. (2010a) 'Temporal Consciousness', Stanford Encyclopedia of Philosophy http://plato.stanford.edu/entries/consciousness-temporal/.

Dainton, B. (2010b) *Time and Space* 2nd edn (Durham: Acumen).

Dainton, B. (2012) 'On Singularities and Simulations', *Journal of Consciousness Studies* 19, pp. 42–85.

Dainton, B. and Bayne, T. (2005) 'Consciousness as a Guide to Personal Persistence', *Australasian Journal of Philosophy* 83 (4), pp. 541–71.

Dennett, D. (1981) 'Where Am I?', in *Brainstorms: Philosophical Essays on Mind and Psychology* (Cambridge, Mass.: MIT Press).

Descartes, R. *Philosophical Writings of Descartes*, eds. J. Cottingham, R. Stoothoff and D. Murdoch (Cambridge: Cambridge University Press, 1984).

Eddington, A. (1928) *The Nature of the Physical World* (London: Macmillan).

Egan, G. (1997) *Diaspora* (London: Gollanz).

Fukuyama, F. (2004) 'Transhumanism', *Foreign Policy*, September/October edition.

Gazzaniga, M. (2005) 'Forty-five Years of Split-brain Research and Still Going Strong', *Nature Reviews Neuroscience* Aug, 6 (8), pp. 653–9.

Good, I. J. (1965) 'Speculations Concerning the First Ultra-intelligent Machine', *Advances in Computing* 6.

Hood, B. (2012) *The Self Illusion* (London: Constable and Robinson).

James, W. (1890) *The Principles of Psychology* (Cambridge, Mass.: Harvard University Press).

James, W. (1904) 'A World of Pure Experience' in *Essays in Radical Empiricism* (Mineola, NY: Dover, 2003).

Johnston, M. (2010) *Surviving Death* (Princeton, NJ: Princeton University Press).

Koch, C. (2009) 'When Does Consciousness Arise in Human Babies? Does Sentience Appear in the Womb, at Birth or During Early Childhood?', *Scientific American*, 2 Sept. 2009.

Locke, J. (1689) *Essay Concerning Human Understanding* (Oxford: Oxford University Press, 1975).

Miller, K. (2004) 'How to be a Conventional Person', *The Monist* 87 (4), pp. 457–74.

Miller, K. (2012) 'Personal Identity Minus the Persons', *Philosophical Studies* 166 (1), pp. 91–109.

Nichols, S. and Bruno, M. (2010) 'Intuitions about personal identity: an empirical study', *Philosophical Psychology* 23 (3), pp. 293–312.

Parfit, D. (1984) *Reasons and Persons* (Oxford: Oxford University Press).

Russell, B. (1927) *The Analysis of Matter* (London: Kegan Paul).

Russell, B. (1948) *Human Knowledge: Its Scope and Limits* (London: George Allen and Unwin).

Sacks, O. (2012) *Hallucinations* (New York: Knopf).

Sandberg, A. and Bostrom, N. (2008) 'Whole Brain Emulation: A Roadmap', Future of the Humanities Institute Technical Report #2008-3, http://www.fhi.ox.ac.uk/brain-emulation-roadmap-report.pdf.

Savulescu, J. and Bostrom, N. (eds.) (2008) *Human Enhancement* (Oxford: Oxford University Press).

Sider, T. (2002) *Four-Dimensionalism* (Oxford: Oxford University Press).

Sternbach, R. and Okuda, M. (1991) *Star Trek: The Next Generation Technical Manual* (Toronto: Pocket Books).

Strawson, G. (2009) *Selves* (Oxford: Oxford University Press).

Strawson, G. (2011) *Locke on Personal Identity: Consciousness and Concernment* (Princeton, NJ: Princeton University Press).

Tononi, G. (2008) 'Consciousness as Integrated Information: A Provisional Manifesto', *Biological Bulletin* Dec, 215 (3), pp. 216–42.

Turing, A. (1950) 'Computing Machinery and Intelligence', *Mind* 59 (236), pp. 433–60.

Vinge, V. (1993) 'The Coming Technological Singularity: How to Survive in the Post-human Era', *Whole Earth Review*, winter edition.

Williams, B. (1970) 'The Self and the Future', *Philosophical Review* 79 (2), pp. 161–80.

Index

air travel, hypersonic 11
ancestor simulation 193–4
animalism 17
Aristotle 25–6, 28, 43
artificial intelligence 149–52,
    185–6
awareness 94–7

Baggini, Julian, *The Ego Trick*
    87–90
Block Universe 206–10
Blum, Andrew 14
Bostrom, Nick 187, 193–4
brain
   as information processor 160
   'missing brain' thought
     experiment 1–4, 37, 101
   neuroscientific
     discoveries 147–8, 152–3
   pineal gland 36–7
   split-brain patients 131–2

Cartesian conception of the
    mind and self. *see*
    Descartes, René
C-continuity 83, 113–15, 191
Chalmers, David 186
  The Conscious Mind 159–61,
    169, 172

co-consciousness 93–4, 98,
    108–10
   diachronic 108–10
computers 152–3, 193–4, 203.
    see also virtual worlds
consciousness. *see also* streams
    of consciousness
   experiential continuity 39,
     60–2, 67
   nature of 8–9, 47–8,
     94–7
   and physical world 153–60
   problem of 8–9
   sleeping souls 72
   unity at a time 92–108
   unity over time 102–12
   and virtual worlds
     186–91
C-phases 80–2
C-systems 74–80, 84–5,
    85–7, 88
C-theory 82–4, 86, 90, 91–2,
    118–21, 168
C-thesis 62–4, 111

Day of Judgment 46
death, and survivability of 9,
    125–6, 183
Dennett, Daniel 4, 37

Descartes, René
  Cartesian soul 33–5
  demonic hypothesis 21–3,
    23–4, 198–9
  'I think, therefore I am' 23
  mind/ body dualism 20–1,
    35–9, 142–3, 146–7, 161–2
  physical world and the mind
    28–30, 32–3, 149, 153–4
  self as immaterial mind 19,
    34–5, 141, 144
  sleeping souls 72
  and virtual worlds 187–8
drones 144–7
drunkenness 146–7
dualism, the scientific argument
    28–33, 153–9
  naturalistic 159–62

Eddington, Arthur, *The Nature
    of the Physical World* 166–8
Egan, Greg, *Diaspora* 190
Ego 97–8, 99, 100–2
Ego Trick 87–9
Ego-centric concern 117–18
Einstein, Albert 209–10
emergence, of consciousness
    155–9
experiential continuity 61–2, 67,
    69, 173
experiential potential (or
    capacity) 76–8, 84–5, 86,
    119–21, 128, 168–9
experiential properties 156–9,
    163–4, 164–8

fission 131–7
forms 25–7
Fukuyama, F. 178–9

Galileo 25, 27–8, 30, 43
games, virtual reality 56–67,
    63–4, 196
ghosts 142–3
Growing Block universe 206

Hood, John, *The Self Illusion*
    87–90
Hume, David 96–7, 99–100
hylomorphic system 26

immaterial minds 19, 34–9, 141,
    144, 145
immaterial self 72
immaterial soul 19, 38, 72, 84,
    112, 127–8, 145–7
immaterial substance 34, 45,
    75–6, 84, 168–9
informational teleportation. *see*
    teleportation
intelligence, and the case for
    dualism 29, 148–53
interaction, problem for dualism
    142–8
intrinsic qualities 156

James, William 98–100, 102–3,
    106–7
Jeopardy (game show) 150
Johnston, Mark 124–5, 127–8,
    135–6, 180

Kurzweil, Ray 183

Locke, John
  *Essay Concerning Human
    Understanding* 30–2, 39–40,
    72–4
  and mental continuity 44+5
  Neo-Lockeans 49–53
  and personal identity 43–7,
    48–9, 62–3
  and the physical world 30–2
  prince-cobbler thought
    experiment 44–5
  rational parrot 41
  and the self 19
  and thinking matter 42–3
  and Thomas Jefferson 39

Meditations on First Philosophy
  (Descartes) 21–3
memory 48–9, 51–3, 89
mental continuity 19, 44–5
metaphysics 16–17
mind/body dualism 4–8,
  35–9, 142–3, 146–7, 161–2
Moravec, Hans 183

nano-technology 85–6
naturalistic dualism 159–62,
  169, 189, 191
Neo-Lockeans 49–53

Parfit, Derek 17–19, 49, 50,
  114–15, 117, 121–3,
  134–5, 137

parrot, rational 41
personal fission 131–7
personal identity 43–7, 48–9,
  62–3
personal time 136–7
phenomenal present 106–11
phenomenal properties 31, 153,
  159, 165
  and emergence 158–9
physical world
  and consciousness 153–60
  Descartes' view 28–30, 32–3,
    149, 153–4
  experiential properties as
    physical in nature 164,
    164–8
  Locke's view 30–2
  mechanical worldview 27–9
physicalism 141–4, 149,
  158–9
Presentism 206–10
properties, primary and
  secondary 31–3, 153, 160
Protean selves 125, 180
psycho-copy 121–3, 128–30,
  181–2, 191
psychological
  connections 50–3
psychological continuity 50–4,
  60–2, 67, 118–21
  and causation 52
  and teleportation 53–4
psychological selves 50,
  90, 181
psychological systems 49–51

psychological-state transfer
    thought experiments 64–9
Pure Ego theory 96–8, 101,
    112, 117–18

Reasons and Persons (Parfit)
    17–19, 114–15
reincarnation 72
Russell, Bertrand 163–6
Russellian monism 163–4, 169,
    188, 191

Sandberg, A. 187
Scan-&-Duplicate device 123,
    128–30
Scholastic Science 25–7, 29
science fiction characters 6,
    40–1, 45
Scientific Revolution 24–33,
    153–6
self. *see also* consciousness;
    lpersonal identity; souls;
    virtual worlds
    biological beings 26, 29, 39
    as conscious 8–9
    as C-system 85–7
    future possibilities 182–3
    illusory 87–8
    as immaterial mind 19, 34–5,
        141, 144, 145
    Locke's concept of 'person'
        40–3
    mind/body dualism 4–8,
        20–1, 35–9, 142–3, 146–7,
        161–2

modes of existence in time
    205
Neo-Lockean view 49–53
Parfit's *Reasons and Persons*
    17–19, 114–15
psychological 90, 181
self-location 38, 101–2
self-oriented concern 118–21
Shoemaker, Sydney 49, 50
simulation argument 194,
    197–204
singularity 186
sleep, dreamless 72, 97
souls. *see also* Descartes, René
    belief in 4–5, 20
    Cartesian 33–5
    sleeping souls 72
speciation 181–3
Star Trek 6, 115–17
Strawson, Galen 166
streams of consciousness
    bearers of change and
        persistence 104–5
    and C-phases 80–2
    and C-systems 78–80
    and C-theory 91–2
    in the future 196–8
    in James's *Principles* 102–3
    and our existence 61–2, 71
    and phenomenal present
        106–11
    and psy-state transfer 68
subjects of experience 71
substantial forms 26, 43
superintelligence 186

teleportation
  and C-continuity 113–15,
    191
  future prospects 179–83
  informational teleportation
    11–17
  personal fission 131–7
  psycho-copies 121–3,
    128–30, 181–2
  and psychological continuity
    53–4, 118–21
  in science fiction 6–7, 45
  Star Trek 6, 115–17
  survivability 17–19, 123–5,
    138
  wormhole travel 139–40
thought experiments
  Descartes' demonic 21–3,
    23–4, 198–9
  methodological rationale 7
  'missing brain' case 1–4, 37,
    101
  prince-cobbler 44–5
  psy-state transfer 64–9
  U-SIM (Ultimate Simulation
    Machine) 57–61, 63–4, 67,
    179, 191
time 136–7, 205–13
time travel 137
Tononi, Giulio 160
transhumanism 177–9,
  184, 190
Turing, Alan 149–50
Turing Test 149–50

unconsciousness, surviving
  it 74
uploading, survivability of
  186–94
U-SIM (Ultimate Simulation
  Machine) thought
  experiment 57–61, 63–4,
  67, 179, 191

vampires 40–3, 75, 170
virtual reality games 56–62,
  63–4, 196
virtual reality, neural
  interfaces 195
virtual worlds
  and consciousness 186–91
  future prospects 9, 183–6
  and heaven 186–8
  simulation argument 194–5,
    200–4
  simulation threat 191–4
  trips to the past 195–8
  upload procedure 189–91
  U-SIM experiment 57–61,
    63–4, 67, 179, 191

website, supporting 213
Williams, Bernard, 'The Self
    and the Future' thought
    experiments 64–9
World of Warcraft 196
wormhole travel 139–40

zombies 170–5, 186, 188, 189